THE

P O P

VOCABULARY
BOOK

NICK CAMAS

Pennhills Press
Seal Beach, CA

Published by Pennhills Press
1077 East Pacific Coast Highway, Suite 122
Seal Beach, California 90740

Distributed to the book trade in the United States by Login Publishers Consortium, 1436 West Randolph, Chicago, Illinois 60607, (800) 626–4330

Distributed in Canada by Fitzhenry & Whiteside, 195 Allstate Parkway, Markham, Ontario L3R4T8, (800) 387–9776

Cover design: George Paturzo
Interior design: Bert Gader
Editor: Robin Quinn

ISBN: 0–9645851–1–1

Library of Congress Cataloguing – In – Publication Number: 95–20276

Manufactured in the United States of America
10 9 8 7 6 5 4 3 2 1

DEDICATION

To my parents

who sacrificed greatly so that I could have so much.

ACKNOWLEDGMENTS

Many thanks to all those whose encouragement, critiques, inspiration and support contributed to the making of this book:

Lauren Layton
Tana Coury
Bruce Chandler
Andy Hall
Bob McMahon
John and Pat Capizzi
Dusti Taylor
Howard Ungerleider
Leslie and Regina Quick
Eric and Marilyn Musgrave
Dave Smith
Cliff Dabney
Scott Von Eps
Joe Grohman
Jim Godwin
Don Rasmussen
Jack Gordon

Paul Moreno
Roy Black
George Kelly
Tom Meador
Charlie and Patty Miskell
Bill Westerlund
Blair Woodward
Jack Kightlinger
Skip Irwin
Bob Westerlund
John Arbeznik
Will Barnes
Robert Slavens
Duane Cecil
Nina Papageorges
Ron Kredell
Lynne Aguirre

Lionel Moore
Suzanne Allen
Pat Cantalupo
Jim Stangeland
David Williams
Janet Day
Michelle Haasl
John and Bobbi Wiggins
Joe and Diane Collins
Thad King
Louise Flanigan
Ed Bohn
Mike Mitchell
Deborah Lundell
Lisa Nelson
Rose Monfore
Erik Bateman

John Seymour
Kristen Miller
Mike and Aana Perkins
Paul Seymour
Jami Reed
Bob Swanson
David Palmer
Robert Barnett
Sheila Posner
Ray Danniels
Lew Zande
Peter Zande
Kathy Hamilton
Jeff Eales
Keith Jettie
Dudley De Zonia
Birgit Rose
Peter Zeughauser
Terry Baysinger
Rick Cicetti
Carlo Tommarello
Erle Halliburton
Rich and Brenda Reilly
Len Geller

Joe Tedesco
Rod Hughes
Pat Dooley
Al Harden
Kari Nelson
Rick Simpson
Gerry Spence
Kevin Laura
George Evans
Rick Dunham
John McLaughlin
William Safire
David Geffen
Joyce Waller
Sara Kinney
Tony Geranios
Brad Faxon
Fred Couples
Paul Azinger
Mark Calcavecchia
Rick Rickerson
Ray Fortune
Brian Krueger
Jack York
Cindy Matthews

Robin Zielan
Jim Bertram
George Edwards
Tiger Woods
Joe Elmer
Mike Powers
Nance Epsteen
Mary Finn
Marcy Alcantra
Bob Vickery
Jan King
Bob Dubill
Jodi Grumet
Janet Amon
Georgianna Halverson
Sharon Hansen
Paul Schafer
Rebecca Taylor
Tim Biehler
Mary Martin
Kristine Jensen
Phil Lauria
Lynn Bryant
Kevin Riley
Matt Sosnowskı

THE FOLLOWING INDIVIDUALS DESERVE SPECIAL ACKNOWLEDGMENT:

To Ron and Marge Franco and their children, Melinda and Jenny, for their gracious hospitality and being there at the outset.

To Jim McGinley for creative and promotional expertise.

To Tom Hedge (one of the brightest, personable people on the planet) who always urged me to just finish the project.

To Mike and Judy Chiariello for strategizing and comic relief.

To record executive, Clive Davis, (he has the "best ears" in the music business), for wit, valuable insights and the willingness to give "talented upstarts" a chance.

To Bill "Bit" Lansdale for wit, wisdom, great stories and many acts of kindness.

To my creative team: George Paturzo – Cover design, Bert Gader – Interior design and Robin Quinn – Editor for being extremely talented, wonderful people to work with.

To my fellow musicians: Trevor Rabin, Geddy Lee, Alex Lifeson, Neil Peart, Edward Van Halen, David Foster, Chris Squire, David Gilmour, Peter Townshend, Roger Daltrey, John Entwistle, Lindsey Buckingham, Chris De Garmo, Pat Benatar, Neil Geraldo, Myron Grombacher, Jimmy Page, Robert Plant, John Paul Jones, Joe Walsh, Rick Wakeman, Geoff Downes, Patrick Moraz, Lou Gramm and Daryl Hall for igniting my energy and maintaining my equilibrium and enthusiasm.

To my family for their prayers, cheerleading and always being there.

To Gary Larsen for "green lighting" the project, constant "brainstorming" and giving the final stamp of approval.

INTRODUCTION

The words in your vocabulary constitute your "building blocks of thought," and they are a vital means to understanding and appreciating various aspects of life experience. Vocabulary proficiency enables you to gain the admiration and respect of teachers, employers and friends.

For the average American, primary vocabulary development ceases after the eighth grade. Essentially, we are "left to our own devices" to develop an intelligent, sophisticated vocabulary, which serves as the foundation to sharing our thoughts with other people.

Last year, I began compiling a list of words and phrases from the mainstream media and my leisurely reading to enhance my vocabulary. Shortly thereafter, I concluded that there wasn't a simple, efficient or effective way to improve one's vocabulary.

Few people would attempt this task by expending countless hours reading a voluminous or pocket–sized dictionary or thesaurus. Such a process would indeed be unduly burdensome and impractical. Furthermore, learning words and expressions from context can be misleading, confusing and frustrating. Learning words using etymology, the history of words, can also be misleading and perplexing. Etymology is mainly helpful to remember words that you already know, but not beneficial to determine the meaning of words that you don't know.

Consequently, following a visit to the World's Largest Bookstore (Toronto, Ontario), I used twelve prominent sources, in addition to the mainstream media, to compile this book. (I sifted through approximately 180,000 words from the prominent sources). Granted, numerous judgment calls had to be made regarding word and phrase inclusions, as well as the number of contextual meanings enumerated.

I decided to combine contemporary, enlightening, humorous words and phrases with selected slang words and expressions to make this book more comprehensive, interesting and entertaining.

Most vocabulary improvement books are very similar in concept, design and structure. I have taken the "word lists with simple meanings approach" so that the reader wouldn't have to search through long, complicated definitions or look up the meaning of words used to define a particular word or phrase.

I strongly recommend that the reader focus on the three following scenarios:

1) words and phrases that are familiar but whose meanings are uncertain;

2) words and phrases that are familiar but whose meanings are completely unknown, and;

3) words and phrases that are completely unknown.

This book will be a valuable resource to enhance your reading comprehension, listening ability and oral and written communication skills.

The book should be especially appealing to those attending college, college–bound individuals and gifted high school students. A strong vocabulary can assist students in writing reports, research papers and examinations, making presentations and eventually interviewing for employment. College students majoring in English, Journalism, Communications or Public Relations will find this book indispensable.

Finally, wordsmiths and other professionals will find this book advantageous in facilitating personal growth and career success.

Learn, implement and enjoy!

PRONUNCIATION NOTE

In this book, pronunciation keys are rendered phonetically. Not all pronunciations of a given word or phrase have been listed for the sake of simplicity. What has been given is the most common accepted means of pronouncing a given word or phrase.

As a guide,
the following vowels are pronounced:

ay – long a
ee – long e
ie – long i
oh – long o
yoo – long u

For the phonetic pronunciations, all syllables are capitalized.

Abbreviations Key

As a guide, the following abbreviations are noted by
the following:

> n. – noun
> vb. – verb
> adj. – adjective
> adv. – adverb
> conj. – conjunction
> interj. – interjection
> prep. – preposition
> pref. – prefix

ab initio- (AB ih-NISH-ee-OO) [Latin] adv. from the beginning

aboveboard-adj., adv. without deceit; straightforward in manner

aboveground-adj. existing within the establishment; conventional

a capella- (AH kuh-PEL-uh) [Latin] adv. without instrumental accompaniment

a

access broker-n. a political lobbyist

Achilles' heel- (uh-KIL-eez) n. a vulnerable spot or area

acronym- (AK-ruh-NIM) n. a word formed from the first letter (or letters) of the words in a set phrase, such as "NATO" from North Atlantic Treaty Organization or "radar" from radio detecting and ranging

acumen- (AK-yuh-mun, uh-KYOO-) n. keenness, accuracy and quickness of judgment or insight; mental sharpness; shrewdness

addendum- (uh-DEN-dum) n. something added

ad hoc- [Latin] adj., adv. for a specific purpose or situation; improvised

ad hominem- (HOM-uh-NEM) [Latin] adj. appealing to emotion and prejudice rather than logic or reason

ad infinitum- (IN-fuh-NIE-tum) [Latin] adj., adv. endlessly; without limit; forever

adiposity- (AD-uh-POS-ih-tee) n. the condition of being fat; obesity

adjunct- (AJ-UNGKT) n. someone or something associated in a dependent or subordinate position

ad nauseam- (NAU-zee-um) [Latin] adv. to a ridiculous or disgusting degree

ado- (uh-DOO) n. trouble; fuss; bother

ad valorem- (AD vuh-LOR-um) [Latin] adj. proportionate to value

advance man-n. a person hired to travel ahead of a politician or theatrical company to arrange publicity, scheduling and security

advocacy journalism-n. journalism in which the writer or publication promotes a particular cause

aegis- (EE-jis) [Greek] n. protection; sponsorship. Also egis.

affectation- (AF-ek-TAY-shun) n. behavior meant to give a false impression; make-believe; posturing

aficionado- (uh-FISH-uh-NAH-doh) [Latin] n. an enthusiastic follower or admirer; a fan or devotee

a fortiori- (AY FOR-tee-OR-ie, FOR-shee-) [Latin] adv. for a stronger reason; all the more

afterclap-n. an unexpected, often unpleasant aftereffect

afterglow-n. the pleasant feeling following an enjoyable experience; an enduring impression of past glory or success

aftermarket-n. the market in replacement parts, repairs and additional equipment related to a manufactured product

agog- (uh-GOG) adj., adv. in a state of eager excitement, interest or curiosity

a

ailurophile- (ay-LOOR-uh-FILE, eye-LOOR-) n. one who loves cats

a la- (AH LUH) [French] prep. in the manner of

a la mode- (AH luh MODE, ALL uh MODE) [French] adj. stylish; in fashion; served
with ice cream

alarmist-n. a person who needlessly alarms or excites others by inventing or
spreading false or exaggerated rumors of forthcoming danger or catastrophe

albatross- (AL-buh-TROS) n. an obstacle to success; a constant, distressing burden

albeit- (all-BEE-it) conj. although; even though; whereas

alfresco- (al-FRES-koh) [Italian] adj., adv. occurring outdoors; in the fresh air; open air

alluring- (uh-LOOR-ing) adj. highly attractive; strongly tempting

alternative school-n. a nontraditional school in educational ideals, curriculum and
teaching methods

amazon- (AM-uh-ZAHN, -zun) n. a tall, physically strong woman

ambience- (AHM-bee-uns) [French] n. a special mood or atmosphere created by a
particular environment

ambrosia- (am-BROH-zhuh) [Latin] n. anything that has a delightful flavor or fragrance

amok- (uh-MUK) adv. in a state of wild excitement, violent agitation or confusion; in an uncontrolled manner

anachronism- (uh-NAK-ruh-NIZ-um) n. anything misdated; something out of its proper time or place

anagram- (AN-uh-GRAM) n. a word or phrase created by rearranging the letters of another word or phrase, such as "satin to stain" and "now to won"

ancillary- (AN-suh-LAIR-ee) adj. subordinate; secondary; serving a supportive function; helping; supplementary

androgynous- (an-DROJ-uh-nus) adj. having both male and female characteristics; unisex

anecdote- (AN-ik-DOTE) n. a brief, entertaining or humorous story of some incident

angst- (AHNGKST) [German] n. a feeling of anxiety or fear which is often accompanied by depression

Annie Oakley-n. (slang) a free ticket or pass

anthromorphism- (AN-thruh-puh-MOR-FIZ-um) n. assignment of human behavior or characteristics to animals, objects or natural phenomena

antidumping-adj. relating to laws or tariffs that raise the prices of imported goods so that they cannot be sold at less than the cost in the country of origin or the cost of similar domestic goods

apish- (AY-pish) adj. foolishly imitative; silly

apocryphal- (uh-POK-ruh-FUL) adj. of questionable authenticity; erroneous; fictitious; counterfeit

apollonian- (AP-uh-LOH-nee-UN) adj. rational, well-ordered and harmonious

apoplectic- (AP-uh-PLEK-tik) adj. very angry; furious; enraged

aposiopesis- (AP-uh-SIE-uh-PEE-sis, AP-oh-SIE-) n. a sudden breaking of a thought in the middle of a sentence, as if the speaker were unable or unwilling to continue

a posteriori- (AY pos-TEER-ee-OR-ie, -ee) [Latin] adj. reasoning from facts to a general conclusion; based on experience

apple-knocker-n. an unsophisticated country person

apple-pie-adj. (slang) nearly perfect

a priori- (AY prie-OR-ie, -pree-OR-ee) [Latin] adj. based on theory rather than experience; not supported by factual study

apropos- (AP-ruh-POH) [French] adj. relevant
adv. by the way

arcane-adj. mysterious; hidden; secret; obscure

archetype- (AR-kuh-TYPE) n. an original model or pattern; a prototype; an ideal
example of a group or kind

argent- (AR-junt) adj. silvery

argumentator- (AR-gyuh-men-TAY-tur) n. a person who generates controversy
or argument

Armageddon- (AR-muh-GED-un) n. a catastrophic conflict; any significant, decisive
battle; the final battle between the forces of good and evil

armchair-adj. removed from active involvement, firsthand experience or
direct investigation

arrant- (AR-unt) adj. plainly or completely such

arrears-(uh-RIRZ) n. unpaid and overdue debts; unfulfilled obligations

arsy-varsy-adj. upside-down, downside-up; completely backwards

artsy-craftsy-adj. decorative rather than functional; pertaining to an interest in arts
and crafts, especially in regard to objects produced as a hobby

artware-n. an artistic medium combining state-of-the-art computer hardware and
software with multimedia applications such as audio, video, television and
light shows

a

assignation- (ASS-ig-NAY-shun) n. something assigned; an appointment made secretly by lovers

astigmatic- (ASS-tig-MAT-ik) adj. having a distorted judgment or view

aswoon- (uh-SWOON) adj., adv. being in a state of great joy or pleasure

at bay-adj., adv. unable to escape; cornered; under control

at large-prep. among the population while being sought by law enforcement

atwitter- (uh-TWIT-ur) adj., adv. nervously concerned or excited

auburn-adj. reddish-brown

auctorial- (ok-TOR-ee-ul) adj. pertaining to an author

aureous- (OR-ee-us) adj. golden in color

auteur- (oh-TUR) [French] n. a film maker or director with a distinctive personal style

azure- (AZH-ur) adj. light purplish-blue; sky-blue

babylonian- (BAB-uh-LOH-nee-un) adj. characterized by extravagance;
        pleasure seeking

bacchanal- (BAK-uh-NALL, - NAL) n. a drunken celebration or festivity;
        a participant in such an event

backdoor-adj. secret; sly

b

backdrop-n. the background or setting of an event

backroom-n. a meeting place used by a secretive controlling group

badinage- (BAH-duh-NAJH) [French] n. teasing conversation

bagatelle- (BAG-uh-TEL) [Italian] n. an insignificant or unimportant thing

baggage-n. unnecessary, dated or burdensome ideas, practices, regulations
    or characteristics

bagman-n. (slang) one who collects money or offers bribes for criminals

bailiwick- (BAY-luh-WIK) n. an individual's specific area of authority, interest or skill

bait and switch-n. a sales tactic using a bargain-priced item or promotional package
    to attract customers who are then encouraged to buy more expensive, similar
    merchandise or services

balderdash-n. nonsense

balkanize- (BALL-kuh-NIZE) vb. to divide a region or territory into small, often
    hostile units

balletomane- (buh-LET-uh-MANE) [French] n. a ballet lover

ballistic- (buh-LIS-tik) adj. explosive; having a short temper

ballyhoo-n. sensational or exaggerated advertising; noisy shouting; an uproar

bamboozle-vb. to deceive; to swindle; to confuse; to puzzle

banana republic-n. a small, politically unstable country that is economically dependent on a single crop or product

band-aid-adj. providing only temporary, insignificant relief

bane-n. the cause of ruin or harm; torment

bankers' hours-n. a short working day

banter-n. good-humored teasing or ridicule

baptism of fire-n. any severe ordeal, especially one that tests a person's courage or strength in a specific area for the first time

barb-n. a cutting or stinging remark

bard-n. a poet; a poet-singer

bare bones-n. (slang) the basic elements or essentials

barfly-n. (slang) a person who spends much time drinking in barrooms

bargain basement-n. a basement floor in a department store where merchandise is sold at reduced prices

b

bargaining chip-n. something used to develop a concession in a negotiation

barmy-adj. foamy; crazy; eccentric

barnburner-n. (slang) a very successful outcome or impressive event

barnstorm-vb. to travel the country giving lectures, performing plays and making political speeches, especially in small towns and rural districts

barrage- (buh-RAHZH) n. an intense, concentrated outpouring of words or attack of blows

basket case-n. (slang) one unable to function properly; anything that doesn't function properly

bastardize- (BAS-tur-DIZE) vb. to lower in quality, character or value

bathos- (BAY-THOS) [Greek] n. a sudden, unintended shift from the lofty to the ordinary; an unintended anticlimax; overuse or repetition in style

battle-ax-n. (slang) a harsh, domineering woman, especially a wife

battle cry-n. a slogan used by the supporters of a cause

bawdry- (BAH-dree) n. obscene or coarse language; lewdness

Bay of Pigs-n. an invasion of another country that results in a total failure

beachcomber-n. a person loitering on beaches who survives by begging or finding things; a seaside vacationer

beaming-adj. shining; bright; cheerful; joyous

bean counter-n. (slang) an accountant

bearish-adj. pessimistic; rude, rough and ill-tempered

beau geste- (boh-ZHEST) [French] n. a gracious gesture, sometimes offered only for effect

bedside manner-n. the attitude and conduct of a physician in a patient's presence

beeline-n. a direct route; a straight line

beleaguer- (bee-LEE-gur) vb. to harass; to trouble persistently; to attack by argument

bel-espirit- (BEL-es-PREE) [French] n. a cultured, intellectual person

bellwether-n. anyone or anything that serves as a leading indicator of future trends

belly-up-adj. (slang) bankrupt

belly wash-n. (slang) a soft drink

benchmark-n. a standard of evaluation, comparison or measurement

b

benighted-adj. morally or intellectually deficient

beyond the pale-adj., adv. with no chance of being accepted or respected by others; in disgrace

big house-n. (slang) a prison

bilge- (BILJ) n. (slang) nonsense; stupid speech or writing

bilk-vb. to cheat; to defraud

billet-doux- (BIL-ay-DOO) [French] n. a love letter

bill of goods-n. (slang) an offer, promise or plan that is dishonest or misleading

bimbo-n. (slang) a silly or stupid person

bird dog-vb. (slang) to follow or observe closely; to seek out talent or clients

bistro- (BEE-stroh, BIS-troh) [French] n. a small restaurant serving wine

bit-n. (slang) a regularly performed entertainment routine; a small part or episode in a theatrical performance; a particular kind of action, behavior or situation

bite the bullet-vb. (slang) to face a painful situation bravely and unemotionally

bittersweet-adj. pleasant and unpleasant at the same time

blackball-vb. to vote against the admission of an applicant to an organization

blank check-n. complete freedom of action

blarney-n. smooth, flattering talk; nonsensical or deceptive talk

blather-n. nonsense; foolish, excessive speech

bleeding heart-n. one regarded as excessively sympathetic to those claiming to be exploited or underprivileged

blind alley-n. a mistaken, unsuccessful undertaking

blind trust-n. a financial arrangement in which a person, such as a public official, avoids possible conflicts of interest by placing personal assets under the control of an independent trustee and giving up the right to information regarding the status of the assets

blip-n. a temporary or insignificant departure from the normal

blitz-n. an intense campaign; a sudden, overwhelming attack

blooper-n. (slang) a clumsy, foolish mistake, especially made in public

blotto-adj. (slang) drunk; intoxicated

blowhard-n. (slang) a loud, bragging or boastful person

b

blowout-n. (slang) a large party, banquet or celebration

blowzy- (BLOU-zee) adj. messy; unkept; bloated and red-faced

blue blood-n. a descendent from the upper class

blue law-n. a law intended to regulate Sunday activities, as in the sale of liquor, retail shopping and entertainment

blue ribbon-adj. outstanding; chosen for special qualifications

blue sky-adj. unrealistic; impractical

bluestocking-n. a woman dedicated to literary or scholarly pursuits

blunt-vb. to make less effective; to weaken

blurb-n. a brief publicity notice, especially one that praises its subject

bodacious- (boh-DAY-shus) adj. remarkable; splendid; bold; gutsy; outstanding in a flamboyant way

bodement- (BOHD-munt) n. a prediction of a future occurrence; an omen

boffo- (BOF-oh) adj. (slang) very successful or popular

bogus- (BOH-gus) adj. false; counterfeit

bohemian- (boh-HEE-mee-un) n. one with artistic or literary interests who lives in a nonconforming, unconventional way

boilerplate-n. a statement reflecting a generally accepted belief or opinion; any of the standard clauses or sections of a legal document

boiler-room-adj. (slang) relating to high pressure, often illegal telephone sales tactics, as in the sale of land, commodities or stocks

bombshell-n. any unexpected, shocking surprise

bona fide- (BOH-nuh FIDE) [Latin] adj. in good faith; authentic

bonding-n. the development of a close, special relationship among family members or friends

bonkers-adj. (slang) crazy; insane; mad

bon mot- (MOH) [French] n. a clever or witty saying

bon vivant- (vee-VAHN) [French] n. one who enjoys superb food and drink and other luxuries

boodle-n. (slang) counterfeit money; money taken as a bribe; stolen goods

bookish-adj. scholarly; well-educated; studious

bookworm-n. one who spends much time reading and studying

boon-n. a timely benefit; a welcomed blessing

boondoggle-n. an unnecessary, wasteful project or expenditure commonly financed by public funds

bootleg-vb. to manufacture or sell illegally

bootstrap-vb. (slang) to succeed without the help of others

bordello- (bor-DEL-oh) [Italian] n. a house of prostitution

bottleneck-n. something that hinders progress or production

boulevardier- (boo-luh-var-DEER) [French] n. a man about town who makes sure to be seen at the trendiest restaurants and clubs

bra burner-n. (slang) a militant woman

braggadocio- (BRAG-uh-DOH-see-OH, -DOH-shoh) [Italian] n. a boastful person; a braggart

brainchild-n. an original idea or plan produced by a person or group

brain drain-n. (slang) the loss of the intellectual, professional and technical resources of a country or region through emigration; the loss of bright employees to competitors

brainstorm-n. a sudden clever idea or plan
> vb. to develop ideas by generating many thoughts and waiting until later to consider their value

brain trust-n. a group of experts who serve, usually unofficially, as advisors and policy planners in government

brannigan- (BRAN-ih-gun) n. a noisy fight; a drinking binge

brasserie- (BRAS-uh-REE, bras-REE) [French] n. a restaurant serving simple meals and beverages

brass ring-n. (slang) an opportunity to attain wealth or success; a prize; a reward

brass tacks-n. (slang) the basics; essential facts

brat pack-n. (slang) a group of highly successful young people working in the same profession

bravado- (bruh-VAH-doh) [Spanish] n. false expressions of courage; boldly resistant or swaggering behavior

bravura- (bruh-VYOOR-uh) [Italian] n. a bold attempt; a display of daring; brilliant style or technique in performing a musical passage

bread and circuses-n. something soothing offered to avoid potential discontent or suffering

breakneck-adj. dangerously fast

breeding ground-n. a place or condition that encourages the development of certain ideas or activities

bric-a-brac-n. (slang) small objects of decoration or curiosity; knickknacks

brickbat-n. (slang) an unfavorable, insulting or critical remark

bridge loan-n. a short-term loan intended to provide or extend financing until a permanent arrangement is made

briefing-n. the act or procedure of giving or receiving pertinent instructions, information or advice

brink-n. at the edge of a steep slope; the point at which something is likely to begin

brinkmanship-n. the policy of gaining an advantage by pursuing a highly dangerous situation to the verge of catastrophe

broach-vb. to introduce; to bring up a subject for discussion or debate

brook-vb. to tolerate; to bear; to put up with something

brouhaha- (BROO-hah-hah) n. an uproar; commotion

browbeat-vb. to intimidate by domineering speech or an overbearing manner

bruin-n. a bear

brush-n. a brief encounter; a short, quick fight; a skirmish

bubble-gum-adj. (slang) displaying an adolescent immaturity in style or taste; bland; dull

bucket shop-n. (slang) a fraudulent securities brokerage operation in which orders to buy and sell are accepted but no executions take place or in which the operators bet secretly against its customers by speculating with funds entrusted to it

buff-n. an enthusiast; a devotee

buffoon- (buh-FOON) n. a clown; a fool

bugaboo- (BUG-uh-BOO) n. a persistent problem; an object of exaggerated anxiety or fear; a source of concern

bugbear-n. anything causing exaggerated anxiety or fear

bug-eyed-adj. (slang) having bulging eyes accompanying a moment of surprise or curiosity

bughouse-n. (slang) a mental health facility

bug juice-n. (slang) a sweet flavored, noncarbonated beverage, such as punch

bullish-adj. optimistic; confident

b

bully pulpit-n. an advantageous position for rallying support or expressing one's views

bumpkin-n. an awkward, unsophisticated individual

bunco-n. (slang) a con game; a swindle

bunk-n. (slang) nonsense

burnish-vb. to polish; to shine

bush league-n. (slang) of inferior quality; second-rate; unprofessional

bushwa- (BOOSH-wuh) n. (slang) nonsense

buttinsky- (but-IN-skee) n. (slang) one who interferes constantly in the affairs of other people

buttonhole-vb. to detain someone in conversation as if by grasping the person's outer garments

button man-n. (slang) a soldier

buzz-n. (slang) gossip; excited talk; a pleasant stimulation from alcohol or other drugs

buzz word-n. (slang) a word or phrase used by members of a specialized field or group that is used chiefly to impress or mystify laypersons

byline-n. a line above a magazine or newspaper article that identifies the writer

byzantine- (BIZ-un-TEEN) adj. highly complicated; not straightforward; scheming

cabal- (kuh-BALL) n. a small group secretly united to promote their own interests or to plot against authority; a secret plot; a conspiracy

cabin fever-n. boredom, distress or uneasiness resulting from a lack of social or environmental stimulation, as when living in a confined space or an isolated area, especially in winter

caboodle- (kuh-BOOD-ul) n. (slang) the entire group, lot or collection

cabotage- (KAB-uh-TAHZH, -TIJ) [French] n. the exclusive right of a country to operate the air traffic within its borders

cache- (KASH) [French] n. a hiding place for food, supplies and valuables; anything hidden or stored in such place; a hidden treasure

cachet- (kuh-SHAY, KASH-ay) [French] n. a mark of distinction, authenticity or individuality; a seal or stamp on a document or letter

cad-n. an unprincipled or ungentlemanly fellow

cagey-adj. careful not to get caught or fooled; crafty; shrewd

cahoots- (kuh-HOOTS) n. (slang) a secret partnership; a questionable association

caitiff- (KAY-tif) n. a despicable, cowardly person

callow- (KAL-ow) adj. lacking maturity; inexperienced

cambist-n. one who is shrewd with money, as a currency trader

camp-n. an appreciation of manners and taste commonly considered vulgar, bizarre, artificial or mediocre

canard- (kuh-NARD) n. a false, deliberately misleading story

c

canned-adj. (slang) completely unoriginal; used repeatedly with little or no change; recorded for radio or television reproduction

canny-adj. cautiously shrewd; skillful; financially prudent

can of worms-n. (slang) a situation that produces successive difficulties as it unfolds; a source of troublesome, unforeseen complexity

capstone-n. the highest point of achievement

cardinal-adj. most important; chief

caricature- (KAIR-ih-kuh-CHUR, -CHOOR) n. a picture or description in which the subject's distinctive features, characteristics or peculiarities are deliberately exaggerated to produce a humorous or distorted effect; an absurdly poor imitation

carouse- (kuh-ROUZ) vb. to partake in noisy, drunken merrymaking

carpetbagger-n. (slang) any politician, promoter or businessperson who seeks success in a new locality because it gives him or her certain advantages

carriage trade-n. wealthy patrons or customers of a business, as of a store, theater or restaurant

carte blanche- (KART BLAHNSH) [French] n. unlimited authority

cash cow-n. (slang) a steady, reliable source of income producing excess funds that are used to finance investment in other areas

catch all-n. anything covering a wide variety of situations

catch-as-catch-can-adj. unplanned; using any means or method

catch phrase-n. a popular phrase serving as a slogan for a group or movement

catch-22-n. a situation characterized by absurdity or senselessness; a self-defeating or contradictory course of action

categorical-adj. absolute; unconditional

category killer-n. (slang) a large retail store chain specializing in a single type of merchandise that is stocked in great quantities and sold at discount prices

catharsis- (kuh-THAR-sis) n. a release of emotional tension that refreshes or restores the spirit

catholic- (KATH-lik, -uh-lik) adj. broad-minded or comprehensive in tastes or views; universal

catty-adj. mean; spiteful; malicious

caucus- (KAU-kus) n. a meeting of members of a political party to determine policy or select leadership; a group within a legislative body seeking to represent a specific interest or influence a certain area of policy

c

cause celebre- (say-LEB-ruh) [Latin] n. any well-known controversy; a famous legal case

cavalier- (KAV-uh-LEER) adj. carefree and unconcerned, especially regarding serious matters; casual; free and easy; egotistical

caveat- (KAH-vee-OT, KAV-ee-OT) [Latin] n. a warning or caution

cavil- (KAV-ul) vb. to find fault unnecessarily; to raise trivial objections

cavort- (kuh-VORT) vb. to bounce or prance about happily

celebrated-adj. well-known; famous; noted

cerebrally challenged-adj. slow-learning

chameleon- (kuh-MEEL-yun, -MEE-lee-un) n. a person of changeable habits or temperament

champion-vb. to support or defend intensely

channel surf-vb. to change television channels with a remote control in search of desired entertainment

chanteuse- (shahn-TOOZ) [French] n. a woman nightclub singer, especially of popular ballads

charade- (shuh-RADE) n. a readily perceived pretense or fiction

charlatan- (SHAR-luh-tun) n. a pretender to having expert skill or knowledge; a quack; an imposter; a fraud

chartreuse- (shar-TROOZ, -TROOS) [French] adj. a pale yellowish-green

chary- (CHAIR-ee) adj. very cautious; watchful

chasm- (KAZ-um) n. a deep hole; a huge gap

cheap-jack-n. a peddler or dealer of cheap, inferior goods

checkered-adj. characterized by great changes in fortune

checkmate-vb. to defeat decisively; to frustrate

cheesy- (CHEE-zee) adj. inferior; poor; cheap

cherry-picking-n. (slang) the practice of buying or investing selectively and carefully with the intent of obtaining a bargain

cherub- (CHAIR-ub) n. a child with a sweet, innocent or chubby face

chic- (SHEEK) [French] adj. smartly stylish or fashionable; sophisticated

chicanery- (shih-KAY-nuh-ree) n. deception; trickery

chichi- (SHEE-shee) [French] adj. very stylish, showy, elegant or sophisticated

c

chintzy- adj. stingy; cheap; trashy; tasteless

chipper-adj. (slang) cheerful; lively

chit-n. a check indicating the amount owed for food and drink

choplogic-n. faulty reasoning; illogical argumentation

chops-n. (slang) the technical skill of a rock or jazz musician

chortle-vb. to laugh joyfully or triumphantly

chromatic- (kroh-MAT-ik) adj. relating to color

chronicle- (KRON-ih-kul) vb. to recount; to record

chrysalis- (KRIS-uh-lis) n. anything in an undeveloped stage

chump-n. (slang) a foolish, stupid or gullible person

churlish-adj. rude; mean; vulgar

chutzpah- (KHOOT-spuh, HOOT-) [Yiddish] n. utter nerve; shameless brashness; gall

cipher- (SIE-fur) n. a person or thing having no value or significance

circa- (SUR-kuh) [Latin] prep. in approximately; about; around

clamjamfry- (clam-JAM-free) n. ordinary people; the masses

claptrap-n. (slang) high-flown nonsense; insincere, showy or empty speech or
      writing intended only to get applause or attention

claque- (KLAK) [French] n. a group of admiring followers or hired applauders at a
      performance

claret- (KLAIR-it) adj. deep purplish-red

clarion- (KLAIR-ee-un) adj. loud, clear and ringing

cliff dweller-n. (slang) a resident of a large, urban apartment house

clip joint-n. (slang) a nightclub, restaurant or other business that regularly
      overcharges customers

clodhopper-n. (slang) a clumsy, stupid person

closet drama-n. a play to be read rather than performed

clubby-adj. (slang) friendly; socially restricted or exclusive as in private clubs

cobble-vb. to put together clumsily or hastily

cockalorum-n. boastful talk; a little man with an exaggerated opinion of his
      own importance

cock-and-bull story-n. an absurd or highly unlikely story told as truth

cocksure-adj. certain; overconfident

coeval- (koh-EE-vul) adj. contemporary; co-existing; of the same age, date or period

cognoscente- (KON-yuh-SHEN-tee, KOG-nuh-) [Latin] n. a person with highly specialized knowledge or refined taste in some field

collateral- (kuh-LAT-ur-ul) adj. serving to support or strengthen; secondary; subordinate

comeuppance- (KUM-UP-uns) n. justly deserved punishment

commandeer- (KOM-un-DEER) vb. to seize forcibly; to confiscate for military or public use

commonweal-n. the public good or welfare

compassionate fare-n. a substantially reduced airline fare for those traveling to attend a funeral or visit someone very ill

conclave-n. a secret or private meeting; a large convention or conference

concubine- (KON-kyuh-BINE) n. a woman who lives with a man although not legally married to him

concupiscence- (kon-KYOO-puh-suns) n. sexual desire; lust

conflagration- (KON-fluh-GRAY-shun) n. a large, destructive fire

confluence- (KON-floo-uns) n. a flowing together of two or more streams;
a gathering point

confrere- (KON-FRAIR) [French] n. a fellow member of a fraternity or profession;
a colleague

congruous- (KONG-groo-us) adj. compatible; harmonious; suitable; appropriate

conniption- (kuh-NIP-shun) n. (slang) a fit of anger, hysteria or panic

connive- (kuh-NIVE) vb. to plot; to scheme; to cooperate secretly in wrongdoing; to
pretend ignorance of wrongdoing

connubial- (kuh-NOO-bee-ul) adj. relating to marriage

consanguinity- (KON-sang-GWIN-ih-tee) n. blood relationship; kinship;
a close connection

consent decree-n. a judicial order obtained by the government which requires a
defendant to terminate illegal activities in return for a dismissal of the charges

consortium- (kun-SOR-tee-um, -shee-um) n. an association of two or more business
or financial entities in a joint venture; a cooperative arrangement among
institutions or groups

constitutional- (KON-stih-TOO-shuh-nul) n. a walk taken regularly for one's health

c

construct- (KON-STRUKT) n. a concept or model; a schematic idea

contentious - (kun-TEN-shus) adj. argumentative; quarrelsome; controversial

contrarian- (kun-TRAIR-ee-un) n. an investor who makes decisions contradicting
the prevailing wisdom, as in buying securities that are unpopular at the time

contretemps- (KON-truh-TAHN) [French] n. an unforeseen occurrence causing
embarrassment or confusion; a misadventure; an accident

contumely- (KON-too-muh-lee) n. insulting rudeness; arrogance; scorn

conundrum- (kuh-NUN-drum) n. a complicated problem or question without a
solution; a brain-teaser; a dilemma

cookie-cutter-n. (slang) pertaining to a project or plan designed according to a
predetermined pattern

coot-n. (slang) an amusing, foolish or eccentric old fellow

coquette- (koh-KET) [French] n. a woman who makes teasing romantic or
sexual overtures

cordon- (KOR-dun) vb. to encircle or close off an area with a posted guard of police,
soldiers or ships

cordon bleu- (BLOO) [French] n. a person highly distinguished in a certain field, as
in a master chef

corinthian- (kuh-RIN-thee-un) n. a luxury-loving person; a wealthy amateur sportsman
adj. elegant; luxurious

corker-n. (slang) an outstanding person or thing

cornpone-adj. (slang) folksy; simple and homey

cornucopia- (KOR-nuh-KOH-pee-uh) n. an abundance of food; an overflowing fullness

corpus juris- [Latin] n. a collection of the laws of a state or nation

cosset- (KOS-it) n. a pet lamb
vb. to pamper; to fuss over

cost-plus-adj. the cost of production plus a fixed rate of profit, as in government contracts with industry

coterie- (KOH-tuh-ree) [French] n. a small, close circle of friends sharing a common interest or background

cottage industry-n. a small-scale business carried on at home; a loosely organized, yet prospering collection of industry or activity

couch-vb. to express a phrase in a particular form or manner; to speak indirectly

couch potato-n. (slang) a person who spends excessive time watching television

c

countermine-vb. to defeat or frustrate by secret measures

coup- (KOO) [French] n. a sudden, successful executed strategy; a brilliant action or move

coup de grâce- (KOO duh GRAHS) [French] n. a decisive event; a finishing act

courtesy card-n. a card entitling the holder to special privileges

coven- (KUV-un) n. a secret plan; a conspiracy

cow college-n. (slang) an agricultural college; a small unknown college in a rural area

cozen- (KUZ-un) vb. to deceive; to cheat; to defraud

crack-adj. (slang) first-rate; excellent

crackbrained-adj. crazy; insane; senseless

crackdown-n. a resorting to strict measures of discipline or punishment; a forceful regulation or restraint

cracker-barrel-adj. (slang) designating the extended, informal discussions on many subjects by people gathered at a country store

crackerjack-adj. (slang) a person or thing of recognized ability or excellence

crank-n. (slang) an irritable, complaining person; an odd person who has stubborn notions about things

crapehanger-n. (slang) a pessimistic or gloomy person

craven- (KRAY-vun) adj. cowardly; fearful

crazy quilt-n. a quilt made of cloth of various colors, shapes, patterns and sizes;
a disorderly mixture

cream puff-n. (slang) a weak, ineffective person; an old, secondhand automobile in
excellent condition

credo- (KREE-doh, KRAY-) [Latin] n. a set of beliefs, principles or opinions; a creed

crestfallen-adj. dejected; depressed; dispirited

crib-vb. to confine; to isolate; to steal; to cheat on schoolwork

crimson- (KRIM-zun) adj. deep red; purplish-red; maroon

critical mass-n. a very important stage; the minimum number or amount required for
something to happen

crocodile tears-n. an insincere display of grief; false tears

crony- (KROH-nee) n. (slang) a long-time close companion or friend

cronyism-n. favoritism shown to close friends without concern for their ability and
qualifications, especially in political appointments

crosscurrent-n. a conflicting opinion, tendency, influence or movement

crossfire-n. a vigorous exchange of opposing opinions or forces; a sudden, heated discussion

crossover-n. a change of musical style to appeal to a larger audience

cross-pollination-n. an inspiration or influence between or among various elements

cross-purpose-n. a conflicting or contrary purpose

crossroads-n. any critical moment or point; a time in which major decisions must be made or important changes occur

crotchety- (KROCH-ih-tee) adj. eccentric; odd; irritable; erratic; changeable

crown jewel-n. a prized corporate asset, especially a highly profitable division of a company desired by another company in a hostile takeover attempt

crucible- (KROO-suh-bul) n. a severe test or experience; an ordeal; a trial; a place, time or situation characterized by the merger of social, economic, political or intellectual forces

cuckold- (KUK-uld) n. a man who is married to an unfaithful wife

cuisine- (kwih-ZEEN, kwee-) [French] n. a style of cooking or preparing food; food prepared at a restaurant

cul-de-sac- (KUL-dih-SAK, KOOL-) [French] n. a dead-end street with a turnaround at the closed end; a situation having no escape; an impasse

cull-vb. to select carefully from among many; to collect; to gather

culture vulture-n. (slang) one who proclaims great interest in the arts or culture

curmudgeon- (kur-MUJ-un) n. a rude, bad-tempered person having stubborn notions and much resentment

curriculum vitae- (kuh-RIK-yuh-lum VIE-tee, VEE-tie) [Latin] n. a summary of one's personal history, education and professional qualifications which is prepared for a potential employer

curry favor-vb. (slang) to seek or gain favor by flattery

curtain call-n. the return of the performers to the stage at the end of a play which is in response to continued applause

cynosure- (SIE-nuh-SHOOR) n. any person or object that is a center of attention or interest

czar- (ZAHR) [Russian] n. a male emperor or monarch; a person having great or unlimited power over others; an appointed official having powers to regulate or supervise an activity

dabble-vb. to undertake something casually or without serious intent

dactyl- (DAK-til) n. a finger or toe

daffy-adj. (slang) foolish; silly; crazy

daisy chain-n. a series of connected activities, events or experiences

dalliance- (DAL-ee-uns) n. playful flirting or toying; a senseless waste of time

darkhorse-n. (slang) a little-known contestant regarded by few as a likely winner

dawdle-vb. to waste time; to loiter; to take more time than necessary

daymare-n. an anxiety attack

deadbeat-n. (slang) one who avoids paying one's debts; a lazy person or loafer

deadpan-adj., adv. (slang) expressionless; emotionless; clearly matter-of-fact, as in behavior or expression

dead reckoning-n. guesswork; predictive calculation

deathtrap-n. an unsafe structure or vehicle; a very dangerous situation

debrief-vb. to question to obtain information or gathered intelligence, especially upon an individual's return from a military mission

debunk-vb. to expose or ridicule as being false or exaggerated

declassé- (DAY-klah-SAY) [French] adj. low-class in appearance, manners, social position or taste; outdated fashion

dedicated tax-n. a tax that, by law, may only be applied to specific uses

deep pocket-n. a source of substantial financial support or wealth

deep-seated-adj. deeply rooted; ingrained; established far within; difficult to remove

d

deep-six-vb. to toss overboard; to get rid of; to discard

de facto- (dih FAK-toh, day-) [Latin] adj. actual
adv. actually; in fact or reality

deft-adj. skillful in an easy, sure and quick manner

defunct- (dih-FUNKT, dee-) adj. dead; inactive

deign- (DANE) vb. to deem worthy; to concede; to see fit

de jure- (dee JOOR-ee, day-) [Latin] adj., adv. legally or rightfully

demagogue- (DEM-uh-GOG) n. a leader who rises to power by appealing to the
emotions and prejudices of the people

demigod-n. a highly honored, respected person

demonize- (DEE-muh-NIZE) vb. to represent as evil

denizen- (DEN-ih-ZUN) n. an inhabitant or resident of; a frequenter of a particular place

denouement- (DAY-noo-MAHN) [French] n. the end result; the final resolution or
outcome of the plot of a literary work

de novo- (dee NOH-voh) [Latin] again; once more

de rigueur- (duh ree-GOER) [French] adj. required by current custom, fashion or manners; socially obligatory

designer drug-n. a drug created with a slightly altered chemical structure to evade prohibitions against illegal substances

desuetude- (DES-wih-TOOD) n. a state of inactivity or disuse

detail man-n. (slang) a pharmaceutical or medical supplies sales representative who calls on doctors, dentists, hospitals and pharmacies

détente- (day-TAHNT) [French] n. an easing of tension or hostility between nations through trade agreements and treaties

devil-may-care-adj. reckless; careless; happy-go-lucky

devoid- (dih-VOID) adj. totally lacking; empty

dewy-eyed-adj. innocent; trustful

dextral- (DEK-strul) adj. relating to or located on the right side; right-handed

diacritical-adj. distinguishing; able to distinguish

diatribe- (DIE-uh-TRIBE) n. an abusive, bitter criticism

dibs-n. (slang) a claim to or rights in something wanted

d

dicey-adj. risky; hazardous

dichotomy- (die-KOT-uh-mee) n. a division into two contrasting sets, groups or classes

dicker-vb. to bargain; to barter

dictum-n. an authoritative, formal statement of fact or principle

didactic- (die-DAK-tik) adj. instructive; morally instructive; included to teach or moralize excessively

diddly-n. (slang) a very small or worthless amount

didymous- (DID-uh-mus) adj. growing in pairs; twin

die-hard-adj. stubbornly resisting change; embracing an apparently outdated or hopeless cause

differential- (DIF-ur-EN-shul) adj. distinguishing; distinctive

digerati- (DIJ-ur-RAH-tee) n. individuals who are highly skilled in the manipulation and processing of digital information

dilatory- (DIL-uh-TOR-ee) adj. delaying; slow; unhurried

dilettante- (DIL-ih-TAHNT) [French] n. an amateur; one having an interest in the arts or another subject only for amusement

dilly-n. (slang) an extraordinary or surprising person, event or thing

diminishing returns-n. a principle of economics holding that a proportionate decrease in productivity occurs after increase in capital, labor or time

diminution- (dih-mih-NOO-shun) n. a reduction or lessening of

din-n. a constant, loud noise

dingus- (DING-us) n. (slang) an article or thing whose name is forgotten or unknown; a gadget

dint-n. effort; a means of

dionysian- (DIE-uh-NISH-un, -NIS-ee-un) adj. wild and sensuous; undisciplined; irrational

diploma mill-n. (slang) an unaccredited school or college that grants worthless diplomas for a fee

dippy-adj. foolish; silly; crazy

dirty laundry-n. (slang) private problems or secrets that could cause distress, embarrassment or gossip if made public

dirty tricks-n. (slang) illegal or unethical tactics in politics designed to destroy the reputation or credibility of one's political opponents; secret intelligence operations designed to disrupt the political situation or economy in another country

d

disaffected-adj. alienated; discontented; dissatisfied

discomfiture- (dis-KUM-fih-CHURE) n. frustration; disappointment; embarrassment

disconcerting- (DIS-kun-SURT-ing) adj. confusing; upsetting; embarrassing

disinformation-n. deliberately misleading information

disingenuous- (DIS-in-JEN-yoo-us) adj. not straightforward; insincere; crafty

dismissive- (dis-MIS-iv) adj. showing disregard or indifference

disquieting-adj. disturbing; troubling; causing uneasiness

dissident- (DIS-ih-dunt) n. a person who disagrees
        adj. disagreeing in belief or opinion

dissolute- (DIS-uh-LOOT) adj. lacking moral restraint; self-indulgent

dissuade- (dih-SWADE) vb. to advise against a course of action by persuasion

distaff-n. women in general; concerns and work considered important to women

dithyramb- (DITH-ih-RAM) n. a very emotional song, speech or writing

ditsy-adj. (slang) silly; disorganized; scatter-brained

ditto-adv. (slang) as before; likewise
      interj. I agree

ditty-n. a short, simple song

diva- (DEE-vuh) [Italian] n. a leading or celebrated female operatic singer

divisive- (dih-VIE-siv) adj. causing discord, disagreement or dissention

divvy- (DIV-ee) vb. (slang) to divide up; to share

docudrama- (DOK-yuh-DRAH-muh) n. a television or movie dramatization of an
      actual event or about real people

doddering- (DOD-ur-ing) adj. senile; feeble; shaky; foolish; silly

doer- (DOO-ur) n. a very active, energetic person

doff-vb. to remove clothing; to put aside; to discard

dog-and-pony show-n. (slang) a detailed, exhaustive presentation of a product or
      policy designed to gain approval

dog days-n. (slang) the hot, humid days of July and August; a period of stagnation

dog-eat-dog-adj. ruthlessly competitive or acquisitive

dogged-adj. stubbornly persistent; untiring; unyielding

d

doggerel- (DOG-ur-ul) n. poorly written poetry, often of a humorous, trivial or ridiculous nature

dog in the manger-n. (slang) a person who selfishly holds onto items that he or she does not need or want in order to prevent others from enjoying or using them

do-gooder-n. (slang) an unsophisticated idealist seeking to cure various social problems in an impractical way

dolce vita- (DOL-chuh, VEE-tuh) [Italian] n. an easygoing life of self-indulgence

dole-n. a charitable distribution of money, food or clothing

dollop- (DOL-up) n. a small quantity; a measure or amount

domo- (DOH-moh) n. (slang) a downwardly mobile professional, who abandons a promising or successful career to focus on more meaningful or spiritual activities

donkey's years-n. (slang) a very long time

donkey-work-n. (slang) hard physical labor, especially if routine or lowly

donnybrook-n. a brawl; an uproar; a free-for-all

doomsayer-n. one who predicts disaster or catastrophe at every opportunity

doormat-n. (slang) one who submits to mistreatment or domination by others

dope sheet-n. (slang) a printed source of information; a program of races at a racetrack

dopester-n. a person who predicts and analyzes trends or future events in sports or politics

do-rag-n. (slang) a bandanna

dossier- (DOS-ee-AY) [French] n. a collection of papers or records giving detailed information about a particular person or subject

dotage- (DOH-tij) n. senility; a deterioration of mental abilities; foolish or excessive affection

doting- (DOH-ting) adj. excessively or foolishly fond of; pampering; senile; feeble-minded

double dipping-n. the practice of receiving two incomes from the government, usually by receiving a pension from prior military service and holding a current government job

double-dip recession-n. an economic concept describing a sequence of a recession, a brief recovery and a subsequent recession

double-entendre- (ahn-TAHN-druh) [French] n. a word or phrase having a double meaning, especially when the second one is indecent or improper

double-minded-adj. undecided; uncertain

doublethink-n. a simultaneous belief in two contradictory ideas

d

double-tongued-adj. deceitful; dishonest

doubting Thomas-n. one who habitually doubts

doughty- (DOW-tee) adj. brave; courageous

dovetail-vb. to combine or connect closely or harmoniously; to correspond

dowdy-adj. untidy; shabby; outdated; old-fashioned

downbeat-n. (slang) a period of inactivity or stagnation

down-market-adj. designed for or appealing to low-income consumers; downscale

downstroke-n. a down payment on a purchase

downswing-n. a decline in business activity

downturn-n. a downward turn in business or economic activity

down under-adv. (slang) in or to Australia or New Zealand

doyen-n. the leader, commander or senior member of a group

draconian- (dray-KOH-nee-un, druh-) adj. drastic; extremely harsh or severe; strict; cruel; inhumane

dramshop-n. a bar or saloon

drawdown-vb. to empty or exhaust the supply of

dreamscape-n. an imaginary dreamlike picture or scene, as in a film

dreck- [Yiddish] n. (slang) trash; rubbish; inferior merchandise

dregs-n. the least desirable part

dressing-down-n. a severe scolding

drippy-adj. annoying; tiresome; overly emotional

drivel- (DRIV-ul) n. senseless or stupid talk

droll-adj. amusingly humorous or odd

drone-n. a lazy or idle person who lives off others; a parasite; a loafer

drool-n. (slang) silly, senseless talk

dross-n. worthless or trivial matter

drumbeater-n. (slang) one who actively supports or publicizes a certain cause

druthers-n. (slang) a choice or preference

dry goods-n. clothing; textiles

d

duck soup-n. (slang) something easy to accomplish; a cinch

duds-n. (slang) clothing; personal belongings

duende- (doo-EN-DAY, DWEN-duh) [Spanish] n. a special quality or charm
to attract others

duffer-n. (slang) an incompetent, ineffective or stupid person; an unskilled golfer

du Jour- (ZHOOR) [French] offered on this day

dulcet- (DUL-sit) adj. sweet-sounding; melodious; having an agreeable,
soothing quality

dumb show-n. (slang) communicating or acting by expressive gestures; pantomime

dun-vb. to ask repeatedly for payment from a debtor
adj. a dull grayish-brown

dupe-n. one who is easily manipulated or deceived

dustup-n. (slang) a fight or quarrel

dweeb-n. (slang) a flunky; a scorned person

dysfunctional- (dis-FUNK-shuh-nul) adj. relating to impaired or abnormal
functioning of a body part or organ; impaired; abnormal

earmark-vb. to set aside or designate for a specific purpose; to put an
   identifying mark on

earnest- (UR-nist) n. money paid in advance to bind an agreement
   adj. serious

eatery-n. (slang) a restaurant

e

ebullient- (ih-BUL-yunt) adj. very enthusiastic; high-spirited; bubbling

éclat- (ay-KLAH, AY-KLAH) [French] n. brilliant success; acclaim; renown

eclectic- (ih-KLEK-tik, ek-LEK-) adj. composed of elements selected from many sources; selecting the best from different sources

economies of scale-n. conditions that encourage mass production of an item by lowering its unit cost as greater quantities are produced

ecru- (EK-roo, AY-kroo) [French] adj. light tan; cream-colored

edacious- (ih-DAY-shus, ee-) adj. greedy; devouring

effete- (ih-FEET) [French] adj. lacking energy, strength or effectiveness; morally deficient

effrontery- (ih-FRUN-tuh-ree) n. boldness; rudeness

egalitarian- (ih-GAL-ih-TAIR-ee-un) adj. characterized by or advocating that all people should have equal social, political, economic and civil rights

Egeria- (ih-JEER-ee-uh, ee-) [Latin] n. a female advisor or companion

eggbeater-n. (slang) a helicopter

egghead-n. (slang) an intellectual

egregious- (ih-GREE-jus) adj. outrageous; extremely bad

eke out- (EEK) vb. to earn a living or supplement with great effort or difficulty

elan- (ay-LAHN) [French] n. enthusiasm; spirited self-assurance; distinctive style

eldritch- (EL-drich) adj. weird; strange

eleemosynary- (el-uh-MOS-uh-NAIR-ee) adj. relating to charity; humanitarian

elephantine- (EL-uh-fun-TEEN, -TINE) adj. gigantic; clumsy; bulky; heavy-footed

elfish-adj. mischievous; prankish

elocution- (EL-uh-KYOO-shun) n. the art of public speaking

elysian- (ih-LIZH-un) adj. relating to paradise; delightful; happy

embattled-adj. troubled by criticism or controversy

embolden-vb. to encourage; to reassure

embracery- (em-BRAY-suh-ree) n. an attempt to influence a change in one's opinion by bribes or threats

emend- (ih-MEND) vb. to improve by critical, scholarly editing

emeritus- (ih-MAIR-ih-tus, ee-MAIR-) [Latin] adj. retired but retaining an honorary position or title corresponding to that held immediately before retirement

éminence grise- (ay-mee-nahns-GREEZ) [French] n. a powerful, influential advisor or decision-maker who operates secretly or informally

emolument- (ih-MALL-yuh-munt) n. compensation for employment

emporium- (em-POR-ee-um) n. a trading center or marketplace; a large retail store

empty nester-n. (slang) a parent whose children have grown up and left home

en bloc- [French] adv. all together

encapsulate- (en-KAP-suh-LATE) vb. to summarize; to condense

enclave- (ON-KLAVE) n. a distinct area enclosed within a larger region

encomium- (en-KOH-mee-um) n. warm, high praise; a formal expression of praise; a tribute

encounter group-n. an unstructured psychotherapy group in which the participants increase their sensitivity, expressiveness, responsiveness and self-awareness by open expression of feelings and touching

endemic- (en-DEM-ik) adj. native to a particular people, locality or region

enervate- (EN-ur-VATE) vb. to weaken or destroy the energy or strength of

en masse- (MASS) [French] adv. all together; in a group

ennui- (ON-wee) [French] n. boredom; dissatisfaction and weariness resulting from a lack of interest

enormity- (ih-NOR-mih-tee) n. an outrageous act; excessive wickedness

ensconce- (en-SKONS) vb. to settle comfortably or securely; to conceal in a secure place

en suite- (on SWEET) [French] adj., adv. in a part of a series or set

entre nous- (ON-truh NOO) [French] adv. confidentially

epicene- (EP-ih-SEEN) adj. having both male and female characteristics

epicure-n. a person devoted to luxurious living and having refined tastes in food and wine

epigone- (EP-ih-GOHN) n. a second-rate follower or imitator of a famous writer or philosopher

epigram-n. a brief, clever saying

epilation- (EP-ih-LAY-shun) n. the loss or removal of hair

epithet- (EP-uh-thet) n. a descriptive term for a person or thing; an abusive word or phrase; a slur

e

eponym- (EP-uh-NIM) n. a person from whom something, such as a city, nation, institution, structure or disease, takes, or is said to take, its name, as in "William Penn" for "Pennsylvania"

ergasiophobia- (air-GAZ-ee-oh-FOH-bee-uh) n. a fear of or reluctance to work

ergo- (UR-goh, AIR-) [Latin] conj. therefore; consequently; hence

eristic- (ih-RIS-tik) adj. provoking controversy; characterized by deceptively convincing argument or reasoning

errant- (AIR-unt) adj. straying from the proper course or standards; wandering in search of adventure; moving aimlessly

erstwhile- adj. former
adv. formerly

erudite- (AIR-yuh-DITE) adj. scholarly; very learned

ersatz- (AIR-ZAHTS, air-) [German] adj. being an inferior substitute; artificial

escape clause-n. a contract clause that specifies the conditions under which the promisor is excused of liability for failure to perform pursuant to the terms of the agreement

eschew- (es-CHOO) vb. to avoid; to shun; to escape

esprit- (eh-SPREE) [French] n. lively intelligence or wit; spirit

espy- (ih-SPY) vb. to catch sight of; to glimpse; to see

ethos- (EE-THOS) [Greek] n. the basic characteristics or values of a person, culture, group, institution or movement

eudaemonia- (YOO-dih-MOH-nee-uh) [Greek] n. happiness or well-being

eugenics- (yoo-JEN-iks) n. the science of improving the human species by controlling the factors influencing heredity

Eurodollars-n. deposits of U.S. dollars in foreign banks, especially in Europe

euthenics- (yoo-THEN-iks) n. the science of improving the human species through control of environmental factors

evanescent- (EV-uh-NES-unt) adj. disappearing like vapor; vanishing

ex cathedra- (kuh-THEE-druh) [Latin] adj., adv. with the authority derived from one's position or office

ex-dividend- adj., adv. designating a period during which a company's shareholders are not entitled to receive a forthcoming dividend

execrable- (EK-sih-kruh-bul) adj. hateful; detestable; very bad or inferior

ex gratia- (GRAY-shee-uh) [Latin] adj. as a favor without legal obligation

e

exit poll-n. a poll taken of a small percentage of voters as they leave a voting location to predict election outcomes regarding the candidates and issues

ex officio- (uh-FISH-ee-OH) [Latin] adj., adv. by virtue of one's office or position

exoteric- (EK-seh-TAIR-ik) adj. popular; suitable for general consumption

ex parte- (PAR-tee) [Latin] adj., adv. from one side only, with the other side absent or unrepresented

exposé- (EKS-poh-ZAY) [French] n. a public disclosure of a crime or scandal

ex post facto- [Latin] adj. enacted or operating retroactively

extant- (EK-stunt, ek-STANT) adj. still in existence

extrapolate- (ik-STRAP-uh-LATE, ek-STRAP-) vb. draw a conclusion based on past evidence; project a trend

eyeball-vb. (slang) to examine or measure carefully; to estimate inexactly by sight

eye-opener-n. (slang) an alcoholic drink taken early in the day; a sudden or shocking revelation or news item

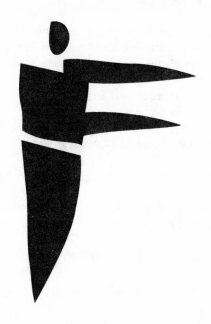

fabulist- (FAB-yuh-list) n. a liar

fait accompli- (FATE uh-kom-PLEE) [Latin] n. an accomplished, irreversible
    deed or fact

falderal-n. nonsense; foolishness. Also folderol.

f

fantabulous- (fan-TAB-yuh-lus) adj. (slang) great; fantastic

fantasia- (fan-TAY-zhuh, -zee-uh) [Italian] n. an improvised, free-form musical composition or literary work structured according to the composer's fancy; a medley of familiar themes or tunes

fantast- (FAN-TAST) n. an impractical dreamer

fanzine- (FAN-zeen) n. an amateur-produced fan magazine that is distributed to a specific subculture or special-interest group

fashion plate-n. one who consistently dresses in the latest fashions

fastuous- (FAST-choo-us) adj. overbearingly self-important or self-glorifying; overdone; high-flown

fatuous- (FATCH-oo-us) adj. complacently foolish; silly or idiotic

faux- (FOH) [French] adj. fake; false; artificial

faux pas- (foh PAH) [French] n. a social blunder

favorite son-n. a candidate favored by the political leaders of his state for nomination as a presidential candidate at a national political convention; a famous man honored and praised by his hometown for his achievements

featherbedding-n. the practice of requiring an employer to hire more workers than
are needed to prevent unemployment or to limit production because of union
rules or safety regulations

featherbrain-n. a flighty, empty-headed or foolish person

febrile- (FEE-bril) adj. feverish; greatly excited

feeding frenzy-n. an opportunity for economic exploitation

fell-vb. to cut or knock down; to kill
adj. cruel; fierce; deadly

femme fatale- (FEM fuh-TAL) [French] n. a charming, seductive woman

fester-vb. to grow embittered; to become an increasing source of irritation or poisoning

finagle- (fuh-NAY-gul) vb. (slang) to obtain, achieve or maneuver by cleverness,
persuasion or deceit; to cheat or swindle

fireball-n. a strong, energetic, forceful person

firebrand-n. one who stirs up trouble or incites a revolt; an agitator

firestorm-n. an intense, often violent disturbance or upheaval; an intense outburst
from many sources

first water-n. the highest rank or quality; the purest luster in diamonds or pearls

f

fizzbo-n. an owner who offers his or her property for sale without using a real estate agent

flack-n. (slang) a press agent

flagging-adj. declining; weakening

flagship-adj. designating the first, finest, largest or most important of its kind

flag-waving-n. efforts to create intense patriotic feelings by deliberately appealing to the emotions; excessive or fanatical patriotism

flannelmouthed-adj. speaking rapidly in a deceptive or insincere manner

flapdoodle-n. (slang) nonsense; foolish talk

flash and trash-n. local television news broadcasts that feature sex, violence and the bizarre to boost ratings

flash point-n. a critical moment at which someone or something bursts forth into significant action, violence or existence

flat-n. an apartment entirely on one floor of a building

flatfoot-n. (slang) a police officer

flatliner-n. a dead person; an idea or product that is dull or inactive

flat tax-n. a tax plan in which all businesses and people would pay the same tax on income from all sources, except unemployment and Social Security benefits

fleabag-n. (slang) a cheap, dirty, run-down hotel

flea-bitten-adj. (slang) shabby; broken down or worn out by long use

flesh out-vb. to fill out or give detail to a framework or structure

fleshpot-n. material comfort; luxury; physical well-being and gratification

flight capital-n. foreign investment in a politically stable country by investors from politically unstable regions

flimflam- n. nonsense; deception; trickery; a swindle

flip-adj. (slang) casually disrespectful or rude; unconcerned; indifferent

flophouse-n. (slang) a cheap, run-down hotel

flounder-vb. to act, move or speak in an awkward, confused manner

fly-by-night-adj. (slang) unreliable; not trustworthy; financially irresponsible

focus group-n. a small group sampled for its emotional response or opinions about a particular subject, especially for market research or political analysis

f

foil-n. a person or thing that by strong contrast emphasizes another's characteristics
vb. to prevent the success of; to frustrate; to confuse or evade

foodie-n. (slang) one having an enthusiastic or refined interest in the preparation
and consumption of fine foods

fool's paradise-n. a state of deceptive happiness or hope, based on illusions

foozle-vb. to manage or perform clumsily; bungle

fop-n. a man overly concerned with his clothes, appearance and manners

foray-n. a sudden attack or raid to seize or steal; a first attempt or venture

forte- (FORT, FOR-TAY) [French] n. something in which one excels

forty winks-n. (slang) a short nap

fossil-n. one who is old-fashioned or has outdated ideas

founder-vb. to fail; to collapse; to sink

fright mail-n. direct mail marketing in which the packaging or envelopes are
designed to appear as if they contain government documents in order
to mislead the recipients and encourage them to open the items

frippery- (FRIP-ur-ee) n. cheap, flashy dress or ornamentation; exaggerated
speech or manners

fritter-vb. to reduce or waste gradually, as in time or money

froufrou- (FROO-FROO) [French] n. fussy or showy dress or decoration

frumpy-adj. unfashionable; dull

fuchsia- (FYOO-shuh) adj. bright purplish-red

fuddy-duddy-n. (slang) a critical, fussy person; an old-fashioned person

funk-n. (slang) a condition of severe depression; cowardly fright or panic

funny money-n. counterfeit money; money from a questionable source

fuscous- (FUS-kus) adj. dark brownish-gray

fustian- (FUS-chun) adj. overdone; self-glorifying

gabble-n. rapid, unclear speech; meaningless chatter

gadabout- (GAD-uh-BOUT) n. a person seeking fun or excitement

gadfly-n. an annoying, critical individual

gaffe- (GAF) [French] n. an embarrassing social blunder

gaga- (GAH-GAH) adj. crazy; foolish; very enthusiastic

gaggle-n. a group or cluster; a flock of geese

gag order-n. a court order prohibiting public commentary or reporting by the news media on a case currently before the court

gag rule-n. a rule limiting or preventing discussion or debate on an issue

gainsay-n. a denial; a contradiction
    vb. to oppose; to speak or act against

gallimaufry- (GAL-uh-MAU-free) n. a jumbled mixture or collection of dissimilar things

gallows humor-n. humorous treatment of a serious or disastrous situation; cynical humor

galoot- (guh-LOOT) n. (slang) a clumsy, unrefined person

galvanize- (GAL-vuh-NIZE) vb. to excite or arouse to action or awareness; to stir

gamut- (GAM-ut) n. the entire range or extent of anything

garb-n. clothing; a manner of style or dress; an external appearance, form or expression

garden variety-adj. ordinary; commonplace

g

garrison finish- (GAIR-ih-son) n. a close finish in a race or contest in which the winner comes from behind at the last moment

gasconade- (GAS-kuh-NADE) n. noisy, boastful talk

gatecrasher-n. a person who enters without being invited or paying

gatefold-n. a book or magazine page that is larger than the normal size and is folded to fit the normal page dimensions

gatekeeper-n. a person who supervises or oversees the actions of others; a person in authority who makes decisions about hiring employees or approving projects

gauche- (GOHSH) [French] adj. socially awkward; unrefined; clumsy

geek-n (slang) any person considered to be different in an odd or negative way, such as being antisocial, stupid, clumsy or tall

geezer-n. (slang) an odd person; an old man; a fellow or guy

gender bender-n. (slang) one who acts or dresses with neither distinguishably masculine or feminine traits

gender illusionist-n. a transvestite; a cross-dresser

Generation X-n. a television programming and marketing category which includes people born after 1965

generic- (juh-NAIR-ik) adj. relating to an entire class or group; having wide application; a product sold without a specific manufacturer's label

genteel- (jen-TEEL) adj. polite; refined; cultured; elegant; fashionable

gentry- (JEN-tree) n. people of high social standing

gerrymander- (JAIR-ee-MAN-dur) vb. to divide a voting area to advance unfairly the interests of a particular political party; to unfairly manipulate in order to gain an advantage

gestalt- (guh-SHTALT) [German] n. the comprehensive view of a situation; the combination of various emotions and experiences that produces a particular feeling

gibberish- (JIB-ur-ish) n. meaningless, unintelligible speech

gimlet-eyed-adj. keenly observant; perceptive

gimp-n. (slang) a person who limps; a limping walk; vigor; fighting spirit

gingerbread-adj. excessive or tasteless decoration

gingerly-adj., adv. very carefully; cautiously

glabrous- (GLAY-brus) adj. bald; smooth

glad hand-n. (slang) a warm, hearty, but often insincere greeting or welcome

g

glad rags-n. (slang) fine or dressy clothes

glasshouse-n. a position, place or situation involving intense public scrutiny

glaucous- (GLOU-kus) adj. bluish or yellowish green

glean-vb. to collect facts or information by patient effort

glib-adj. speaking easily and smoothly but often insincerely

glimmer-n. a faint suggestion or indication; a dim flicker or flash of light

glitch-n. an error or malfunction

glitterati- (GLIT-uh-RAH-tee) [Latin] n. (slang) very fashionable celebrities;
     the smart set

globetrot-vb. to travel widely and frequently, especially for sightseeing

glom-vb. to look or stare at; to steal; to seize

G-Man-n. an FBI agent

gnome- (NOME) n. a dwarf; a wise, meaningful saying

goad-vb. to stir up; to urge on; to stimulate

goat-n. (slang) a scapegoat; a lustful man

gobbledygook- (GOB-ul-dee-GOOK) n. (slang) unclear, unintelligible, wordy speech

godsend-n. something that unexpectedly fulfills one's needs or desires

gofer- (GOH-fur) n. (slang) an employee who performs minor or lowly tasks such as running errands

goldbrick-n. (slang) a person who tries to avoid work or duties; a loafer; anything worthless represented as being genuine or valuable

golden handcuffs-n. (slang) a lucrative incentive to an executive which is intended to discourage resignation

golden handshake-n. (slang) a lucrative payment offered to influence an employee to retire early

golden parachute-n. (slang) an employment agreement that guarantees a top executive lucrative severance benefits if he or she is terminated as a result of a corporate acquisition

gonzo-adj. (slang) crazy; foolish; bizarre; unrestrained

goo-n. (slang) any sticky substance; an excessive or insincere display of emotion

goodfella-n. (slang) a gangster, especially a Mafia member

good old boy-n. (slang) a man characterized as friendly, easygoing, and masculine who strongly identifies with his regional lifestyle

g

goodwill-n. an intangible asset reflecting the value added to a business enterprise
as a result of reputation or patronage; a good relationship of a nation
with other nations

goofball-n. (slang) a foolish, stupid or incompetent individual

goombah- (GOOM-bah) [Italian] n. (slang) an older man who acts as an advisor,
friend or protector

goon-n. (slang) a hoodlum or thug; a stupid person

Gordian knot- (GOR-dee-un) n. any complex problem solved only by drastic measures

gossamer- (GOS-uh-mur) n. any flimsy, delicate substance

gourmand- (goor-MAHND) [French] n. a person who takes hearty, excessive
pleasure in eating

governess- (GUV-ur-nis) n. a woman employed in a private home to educate and
care for children

grab bag-n. (slang) a miscellaneous collection; a package which is selected or
purchased without knowledge of its contents

gracile- (GRAS-il) adj. slender and graceful

grammalogue- (GRAM-ah-log) n. any letter or symbol which signifies a word, such
as "$" for dollars or "&" for and

grandfather clause-n. a clause in a statute that exempts those already involved in a regulated activity or business from the new regulations established by the statute

grandiloquent- (gran-DIL-uh-kwunt) adj. using overblown, self-important words and expressions

grandstanding-n. acting in an unnecessarily showy manner to impress others or win applause

granny flat-n. a rental apartment built onto an existing residential property, originally designed to house the parents or grandparents of the home's residents

grapevine-n. an informal means of receiving or spreading information, rumor or gossip from one person to another; an unrevealed source of confidential information

gratis- (GRAT-is, GRAH-tis) [Latin] adj. free; without charge

gravamen- (gruh-VAY-men) n. the main part of an accusation or complaint; a grievance

Gravel Gerty-n. an underground bunker designed for the temporary storage and disassembly of deactivated nuclear weapons

graveyard shift-n. (slang) an nighttime work shift usually starting at midnight

gravy-n. (slang) money or another benefit easily or illegally obtained

g

gravy train-n. (slang) an occupation or other source of income requiring little effort, while generating substantial profits

gray market-n. a market for the buying and selling of imported goods at prices below those set by an official regulatory agency

gray matter-n. (slang) brains; intellectual capabilities

grease-vb. (slang) to influence by giving money; to facilitate the progress of

greasepaint-n. theatrical make-up

green-eyed-adj. jealous

greenhorn-n. (slang) a beginner or inexperienced person; a person easily fooled

green light-n. (slang) permission to proceed

green marketing-n. marketing efforts by large corporations to persuade the public that their products, manufacturing methods, packaging and intentions are environmentally responsible

gridlock-n. a total lack of progress or movement

grill-vb. (slang) to question or cross-examine closely and persistently

grim reaper-n. (slang) one who is a severe cutter or eliminator of costs, compensation or benefits

griseous- (GRIZ-ee-us, GRIS-) adj. grayish

grit-n. great courage; brave perseverance

grog-n. any alcoholic liquor

groundswell-n. a rapidly growing wave of public opinion

grouse-vb. to complain; to grumble

grubstake-n. money or assistance advanced for any venture in return for a promised share of the profits

grunt-n. (slang) a person who does boring or routine tasks; a footsoldier in the U.S. Military

gudgeon- (GUJ-un) n. (slang) an easily-fooled person

guerilla marketing-n. a nontraditional, direct marketing tactic whereby product samples are handed out, immediate feedback recorded, consumer questions answered, and good public relations established

guff-n. (slang) nonsense; brash or disrespectful speech

guffaw- (guh-FAW) n. a loud burst of laughter

guidepost-n. anything serving as an example, guide or standard; a guideline

g

gumshoes-n. (slang) a detective; an investigator

gunboat diplomacy-n. diplomacy involving intimidation through the threat or use of military force

guru- (GOO-roo, GOOR-oo) n. a recognized leader in a certain field; a trusted advisor; a spiritual and philosophical advisor or teacher

gushy-adj. overly enthusiastic or sentimental

gussy-vb. to dress up; to decorate

gusto-n. hearty enjoyment; enthusiastic appreciation; zest; vigor; liveliness

gut course-n. (slang) an easy, undemanding academic course of study

gutsy-adj. (slang) courageous; daring; forceful and uninhibited

gym rat-n. (slang) one whose dedication and hard work demonstrates an intense determination to succeed at all costs

gyp joint-n. (slang) a business that habitually cheats or overcharges its customers

hack-n. (slang) one hired to do routine or unpleasant tasks; a completely devoted
worker for a political party, who is hired through patronage; a writer who
uses worn-out ideas and expressions; a taxi driver

hacker-n. an unskilled golfer or tennis player; a computer user who illegally
gains access to another's electronic system to obtain secret information
or steal money

hackneyed- (HAK-need) adj. made commonplace by overuse; overdone; unimaginative

h

haecceity- (hek-SEE-uh-tee) n. uniqueness of a particular person or thing; individuality

haggle-vb. to argue about price or terms in a mean, petty way

hagridden-adj. harassed or tormented by irrational fears

halcyon- (HAL-see-un) adj. calm; peaceful; prosperous; golden

half-baked-adj. (slang) insufficiently planned or thought out; ill-conceived; lacking common sense, experience or intelligence

half-cocked-vb. to act or speak too hastily
adj. (slang) inadequately or poorly prepared

hamstring-vb. to impair; to disable; to make ineffective; to frustrate

hand-to-mouth-adj. having or providing the barest livelihood or support

hangdog-adj. guilty; disgraced; ashamed; downcast

happenstance-n. (slang) a chance occurrence; a fluke; an accident

harangue- (huh-RANG) n. a lengthy, loud, scolding speech, especially delivered in a public setting

hard-line-adj. firm and uncompromising in attitude, position or policy

harebrained-adj. foolish; silly; flighty; scatter-brained

harried- (HAIR-eed) adj. pressured; overworked; worried; harassed

harrowing- (HAIR-oh-ing) adj. agonizing; disturbing; distressing

harrumph- (huh-RUMF) vb. to complain or protest in an overblown, self-righteous way; to make brief, critical remarks

harum-scarum- (HAIR-um-SKAIR-um) adj. irresponsible; reckless

hatchet job-n. (slang) a biased, vicious verbal attack on someone's actions or character

hatchet man-n. (slang) a professional killer; one hired to carry out an unpleasant or unprincipled task; a harsh critic or writer who tries to destroy one's reputation

haunting-adj. recurring to the mind; unforgettable

haute couture- (OAT koo-TOOR, -CHOOR) [French] n. the leading designers of exclusive fashions for women and their creations; high fashion

haute cuisine- (OAT kwih-ZEEN) [French] n. the preparation of fine food by highly skilled chefs and the food so prepared

havoc- (HAV-ik) n. destruction; devastation; chaos; confusion

hazel- (HAY-zul) adj. yellowish-brown

heady-adj. shrewd; clever; exciting; reckless; stubborn

h

hebetude- (HEB-ih-TOOD) n. mental dullness or laziness

hegemony- (hih-JEM-uh-nee, HEJ-uh-MOH-nee) n. dominance or leadership of one nation over another

hegira- (hih-JIE-ruh, HEJ-ur-uh) [Latin] n. a journey or trip to escape a dangerous or undesirable situation

heliotrope- (HEEL-yuh-TROPE, HEE-lee-uh-) adj. reddish-purple

hellacious- (heh-LAY-shus) adj. (slang) very bad; unbearable; remarkable; extraordinary

hell-bent-adj. (slang) recklessly eager or determined; firmly resolved; moving very fast or recklessly

hellion- (HEL-yun) n. (slang) a wild, mischievous troublemaker

henchman- n. a loyal, trusted follower or helper; one who supports a political figure mainly for personal gain; a member of a criminal gang

henna-adj. reddish-brown

henpeck-vb. (slang) to harass or dominate by constant nagging

het up-adj. (slang) angry; excited

hibernian- (hie-BUR-nee-un) adj. relating to or characteristic of the Irish or Ireland

hidebound-adj. stubbornly narrow-minded or inflexible; bigoted

highbinder-n. a corrupt politician

highbrow-n. (slang) an intellectual or highly cultured person

high concept-adj. relating to a motion picture whose main idea can be easily summarized in one sentence

high-flown-adj. exceedingly ambitious or aspiring; high sounding but meaningless

highhanded-adj. arrogant; overbearing; arbitrary

high jinks-n. horseplay; lively pranks; playful, rowdy activity

high-minded-adj. having or showing high ideals, principles or behavior; noble

highroad-n. an easy or sure way; the most diplomatic, optimistic or positive course

high-tail-vb. (slang) to leave or go in a hurry, especially when escaping

high tide-n. a climax; the highest point of degree or intensity

high time-n. (slang) an exciting, lively, enjoyable time; the moment just before it is too late

high-water mark-n. the highest point of achievement

h

high wire-n. (slang) a risky operation or job

histrionic- (HIS-tree-ON-ik) adj. overly dramatic; theatrical; pertaining to actors
or acting

hobbyhorse-n. a favorite topic or hobby

hobnob-vb. to associate in a friendly way; to be on close terms

hodgepodge- (HOJ-POJ) n. any jumbled mixture or collection; a medley

hogheaven-n. (slang) a state of complete happiness or contentment

hog-tie-vb. (slang) to make someone or something ineffective or helpless

hoi polloi- (HOY puh-LOY) [Greek] n. the common people; the masses

hoity-toity- (HOY-tee-TOY-tee) adj. conceited; snobbish

hokey pokey-n. deception; trickery

hokum- (HOH-kum) n. (slang) nonsense

hole-and-corner-adj. conducted secretly; kept secret to avoid blame or punishment

holier-than-thou-adj. self-righteous to an annoying degree; displaying an attitude
of superior virtue

homespun-adj. plain and simple; unsophisticated

homunculus- (hoh-MUN-KYOO-lus) n. a little man; a dwarf

hondle-vb. (slang) to argue or bargain in a mean, petty way

honeymoon-n. a brief, early period of harmony in any relationship

hoopla-n. (slang) noisy commotion; great excitement; exaggerated or misleading publicity

hoosegow-n. (slang) a jail or prison

hoot-n. (slang) a very funny person; a loud shout of disapproval or scorn

hornet's nest-n. (slang) a situation filled with controversy, hostility, risk or trouble

hospice- (HOS-pis) n. a homelike facility that provides care for the emotional and medical needs of terminally ill patients

hotbed-n. an environment favoring rapid growth or extensive activity

hot button-n. (slang) something that generates an immediate reaction or predictable response to a marketing tactic or a political issue; something of great interest that produces an immediate reaction or predictable response

hotchpotch-n. a random collection; a jumbled mixture; a thick stew of different meats and vegetables

hot potato-n. (slang) an issue or problem that no one wants to handle because of its controversial or sensitive nature

h

hot seat-n. (slang) any difficult position subjecting one to criticism, discomfort, harassment or stress

hotspur-n. a quick-tempered, reckless individual easily disposed to violence

house of cards-n. (slang) an unconvincing or ineffective plan

hubbub-n. noisy confusion or uproar

hubris- (HYOO-bris) n. excessive pride or self-confidence

huckster-n. (slang) a peddler of goods as in fruits and vegetables; an aggressive merchant who uses questionable methods; an advertising copywriter for radio or television

hue and cry-n. a loud, public outcry or protest

huff-n. a fit of sudden anger or irritation

huggermugger-n. disorder; confusion; secrecy; concealment

hullabaloo- (HUL-uh-buh-LOO) n. noisy confusion or excitement; an uproar

hurl-vb. to utter intensely or passionately; (slang) to vomit

hyperbole- (hie-PUR-buh-lee) n. exaggeration; overstatement

icebreaker-n. something said or done to relax a tense atmosphere or situation; a
beginning or start

iceman-n. (slang) a hired killer

icon- (EYE-KON) n. an image; a symbol; a person who is the object of great attention
and devotion; an idol

iconoclast- (eye-KON-uh-KLAST) n. a person who attacks and tries to destroy popular or traditional beliefs or institutions

ideology- (EYE-dee-ALL-uh-jee, ID-ee-) n. the doctrines and beliefs that constitute the basis of an economic, political or social system

idyllic- (eye-DIL-ik) adj. simple and pleasing; picturesque; naturally peaceful; romantic

ilk-n. a kind or type; a class; a family or regional group

illusory- (ih-LOO-suh-ree, -zuh-ree) adj. misleading; deceptive; not real

illustrious- (ih-LUS-tree-us) adj. famous; noted; very clear; evident

imbroglio- (im-BROHL-yoh) [Italian] n. a difficult or complicated situation; a complicated misunderstanding or disagreement; a state of confusion

imbue- (im-BYOO) vb. to inspire or instill with ideas, emotions or principles; to saturate with a dye or stain

imp-n. a naughty or mischievous child

impacted-adj. financially strained by a heavy demand on public services, as in schools and health care

impassioned- (im-PASH-und) adj. passionate; showing strong feeling; overeager

imperious- (im-PEER-ee-us) adj. extremely overbearing or domineering; urgent

impetuous- (im-PECH-oo-us) adj. impulsive and passionate; raging; powerful

impetus- (IM-puh-tus) n. a driving force; a motive; an impulse; momentum

implacable- (im-PLAK-uh-bul, -PLAY-kuh-bul) adj. incapable of making calm or peaceful; inflexible; unsympathetic; heartless

impolitic- (im-POL-ih-tik) adj. unwise; disadvantageous; unsuitable

importune- (IM-por-TOON) vb. to beg or appeal with great persistence and intensity

impregnable- (im-PREG-nuh-bul) adj. difficult or impossible to attack or challenge; unconquerable; unyielding

impresario- (IM-prih-SAR-ee-OH) [Italian] n. a producer or manager of public entertainment, as in an opera or ballet company or concert series

imprest- n. a loan or advance of money

imprimatur- (IM-prih-MAH-tur, -toor) n. official approval or its symbol; official permission to print or publish

improvident- (im-PROV-uh-dunt) adj. wasteful; careless; unmindful

impudent- (IM-pyuh-dunt) adj. bold; brash; shameless; disrespectful

impugn- (im-PYOON) vb. to dispute the truth of; to attack as false by criticism or argument

impunity- (im-PYOO-nih-tee) n. freedom from punishment, penalty or harm

impute- (im-PYOOT) vb. to accuse or charge another with fault or misconduct; to attribute or credit

in absentia- (ab-sen-shuh, -shee-uh) [Latin] adv. in absence; although not present

inane- (ih-NANE) adj. pointless; ridiculous; senseless; silly

in camera- [Latin] adv. in closed or secret session; privately

incendiary- (in-SEN-dee-AIR-ee) adj. causing or capable of causing fire; tending to cause riot or rebellion; arousing strong or violent emotions

incestuous- (in-SES-choo-us) adj. being too closely involved with

inchoate- (in-KOH-it, -ate) adj. just begun; incomplete; unorganized; disorderly

incipient- (in-SIP-ee-unt) adj. just beginning to appear or occur

incognito- (IN-kog-NEE-toh) [Latin] adj., adv. with true identity disguised or concealed

incommunicado- (IN-kuh-MYOO-nih-KAH-doh) [Latin] adj., adv. unwilling or not allowed to communicate with others

incondite- (in-KON-dit, -DITE) adj. poorly constructed; lacking refinement; crude

incongruous- (in-KONG-groo-us) adj. inconsistent; incompatible; inappropriate

incontrovertible- (IN-kon-truh-VUR-tuh-bul) adj. indisputable; unquestionable; undeniable

incorrigible- (in-KOR-ih-juh-bul) adj. incapable of being improved, corrected or reformed; firmly established

incredulous- (in-KREJ-uh-lus) adj. disbelieving; skeptical; doubting

inculcate- (in-KUL-KATE, IN-kul-) vb. to teach by frequent repetition, instruction or urging

incumbent- (in-KUM-bunt) adj. necessary; mandatory; currently holding a particular office

indecorous- (in-DEK-ur-us) adj. lacking good taste or proper social behavior; unrefined; unmannerly

indefatigable- (IN-dih-FAT-ih-guh-bul) n. tireless; persevering

indicia- (in-DISH-uh, -DISH-ee-uh) [Latin] n. identifying or characteristic marks; an envelope marking which serves as a substitute for a stamp or regular cancellation

indolent- (IN-duh-lunt) adj. lazy; idle

indurate- (IN-duh-RATE, -doo-RATE) vb. to make or become unfeeling

ineffable- (in-EF-uh-bul) adj. incapable of expressing in words; undescribable

inexorable- (in-EK-sur-uh-bul) adj. unyielding; inflexible; inevitable; unavoidable

in extremis- (ek-STREE-mis) [Latin] adv. at the point of death; in extreme circumstances

infantile- (IN-fun-TILE, IN-fun-til) adj. childish; immature; in the earliest stage of development

infidel- (IN-fih-dul, -DEL) n. a person who does not believe in or doubts a particular religion, system or principle

inflammatory- (in-FLAM-uh-TOR-ee) adj. tending to cause or arouse strong emotion, such as anger, excitement, passion, rioting or violence

infrangible- (in-FRAN-juh-bul) adj. indestructible; indivisible; incapable of being violated

ingênue- (AHN-zhuh-NOO) [French] n. an innocent, unsophisticated girl or young woman

ingenuous- (in-JEN-YOO-us) adj. simple; unsophisticated; sincere; straightforward

ingrate- (IN-GRATE) n. an ungrateful person

ingratiate- (in-GRAY-shee-ATE) vb. to become popular or gain favor with others by deliberate effort; charm

inkling-n. a slight hint or indication; an indirect suggestion; a vague idea or notion; suspicion

in lieu of- (LOO) [French] prep. instead of; in place of

in loco parentis- (LOH-koh puh-REN-tis) [Latin] adv. in the place of a parent or a parent's authority

inner circle-n. a small, select group of people who influence or control thought or customs

innervate- (IN-ur-VATE) vb. to stimulate to action or movement

innuendo- (IN-yoo-EN-doh) n. an indirect remark or reference that is usually not complimentary

inscrutable- (in-SKROO-tuh-bul) adj. difficult to interpret or understand; incomprehensible; mysterious

insentient- (in-SEN-shunt) adj. unconscious; lifeless; unfeeling

insolent- (IN-suh-lunt) adj. boldly rude or disrespectful; insulting; arrogant

insoluble- (in-SOL-YOO-bul) adj. unsolvable; unexplainable; unable to be dissolved

insouciant- (in-SOO-see-unt) adj. carefree; unconcerned; easygoing

institutional- (IN-stih-TOO-shuh-nul) adj. uniform; established; dull; unimaginative

insufferable- (in-SUF-ur-uh-bul) adj. unbearable; intolerable

insular- (IN-suh-lur, -SOO-lur) adj. isolated; detached; narrow-minded

intelligentsia- (in-TEL-uh-JENT-see-uh) [Latin] n. the intellectuals and enlightened
    class of a society

inter alia- (AH-lee-uh) [Latin] adv. among other things

interdict- vb. to prohibit or forbid authoritatively; to restrain from doing or using
    something

interim-n. a time between events or periods; the meantime
    adj. temporary

interlocking directorates-n. boards of directors of corporations that have common
    directors so that such corporations are practically under the same control

interlocutory- (IN-tur-LOK-yuh-TOR-ee) decided during the course of a lawsuit
    and temporary in effect; conversational

interloper- (IN-tur-LOH-pur) n. an intruder; a person who interferes in another's
    affairs; a trespasser

internecine- (IN-tur-NES-EEN, -NES-in) adj. mutually destructive or harmful

interpolate- (in-TUR-puh-LATE) vb. to insert between other parts; to introduce new
    material into a text

inter vivos- (VEE-VOHS, VIE-) [Latin] adj. between living persons

intestate- (in-TES-TATE) [Latin] adj. having made no legal will; not settled by a legal will

intimate- (IN-tuh-MATE) vb. to hint; to suggest

intractable- (in-TRAK-tuh-bul) adj. stubborn; uncontrollable; disobedient; difficult to remedy or cure

intransigent- (in-TRAN-sih-junt) adj. stubborn; uncompromising; unyielding

intrusive- (in-TROO-siv) adj. interfering; disturbing; annoying; nosy

inure- (in-YOOR) vb. to become accustomed to or hardened by difficulty, hardship or pain; to take effect or come into use

invective- (in-VEK-tiv) n. abusive or insulting speech; strong criticism; an intense verbal attack

inveigh- (in-VAY) vb. to strongly protest; to give angry disapproval; to denounce

inveigle- (in-VAY-gul, -VEE-gul) vb. to obtain or win over by flattery, coaxing or deception

inveterate- (in-VET-ur-it) adj. deep-rooted; long-established; habitual; chronic

invidious- (in-VID-ee-us) adj. causing resentment, ill will or hostility; harmful; destructive

in vitro- (VEE-troh) [Latin] adj., adv. isolated and maintained in an artificial environment outside the living organism

ipse dixit- (IP-see DIK-sit) [Latin] n. an unproved assertion which is based solely on the authority of a quoted source; an arbitrary or dogmatic statement

ipso facto- (IP-so FAK-toh) [Latin] adv. by the fact itself; by that very fact or act

irascible- (ih-RAS-uh-bul) adj. irritable; easily angered; quick-tempered

ire- (EYEUR) n. anger; rage; ill will

irenic- (eye-REN-ik, eye-REE-nik) adj. peaceful; calm; gentle

irksome- (URK-sum) adj. annoying; irritating; tiresome

iron horse- n. (slang) a railroad locomotive

irreparable- (ih-REP-ur-uh-bul) adj. unable to be repaired, amended or corrected

irrepressible- (IR-ih-PRES-uh-bul) adj. difficult or impossible to restrain or control; unmanageable

irresolute- (ih-REZ-uh-LOOT) adj. indecisive; hesitant

itinerant- (eye-TIN-ur-unt) adj. wandering or traveling from place to place to work; roving; unsettled

ivory tower-n. a place or attitude of mental retreat from action and reality; a preoccupation with notable, remote or intellectual matters rather than basic everyday life

jabber-n. rapid or nonsensical talk

jabberwocky- (JAB-ur-WOK-ee) n. nonsensical speech or writing

jacinth- (JAY-sinth, JAS-inth) adj. reddish-orange

jackal- (JAK-ul) n. a cheat or swindler; one who performs lowly tasks for another

jackbooted-adj. cruelly and violently unjust

jaded- (JAY-did) adj. tired; worn-out; indifferent or dulled by excess; cynically unfeeling

jag-n. (slang) a period of uncontrolled drinking, drug use or other activity; a binge

jailbird-n. (slang) a prisoner or an ex-convict; a habitual lawbreaker

jailhouse lawyer-n. (slang) a prisoner who is usually self-taught in the law and gives legal advice to other prisoners

jarhead-n. (slang) a U.S. Marine

jasmine- (JAZ-min, JAS-) adj. pale yellow

jaundiced- (JON-dist) adj. yellowish; displaying hostility, envy or prejudice

jaunty- (JON-tee) adj. fashionable; stylish; self-confident; carefree

jawbone-vb. to try to persuade or pressure by using one's high position or office

jawbreaker-n. (slang) a word that is difficult to pronounce

jejune- (juh-JOON) adj. dull; uninteresting; immature; childish; deficient in nutritional value

jerry-built-adj. built poorly using cheap materials

j

jetsam- (JET-sum) n. discarded cargo and equipment washed ashore; discarded odds and ends

jettison- (JET-uh-zun) vb. to discard something as burdensome or unwanted; to throw overboard or discard in an emergency

jibe-vb. (slang) to agree; to be in accord

jimjams-n. (slang) the jitters; a fit of nervousness

jingoism- (JING-goh-IZ-um) n. extreme patriotism that favors an aggressive, threatening, warlike foreign policy

jive-n. (slang) exaggerated, misleading talk; jazz music

job lock-n. a situation in which a person remains in an undesirable job solely to have health insurance

jockey-n. (slang) one who operates a particular machine, device or vehicle
vb. to direct or maneuver for advantage or position

jocular- (JOK-yuh-lur) adj. joking; humorous; playful

joey-n. a baby kangaroo; any young animal

Jonah- (JOH-nuh) n. one perceived to bring bad luck by being present

journalese- (JUR-nuh-LEEZ) n. the style of writing for magazines and newspapers characterized by the use of cliches and sensationalism

juggernaut- (JUG-ur-NOT) n. a massive, destructive force or object that destroys everything in its way

jugular- (JUG-yuh-lur) n. the most important part

juke joint-n. (slang) a bar or tavern featuring drinking and dancing with music played on a jukebox

jumble-n. a confused, disordered mixture or heap; a disordered state

jumping-off place-n. a very remote place; the starting point for a trip or venture

jump-start-vb. (slang) to begin or set in motion a stalled or sluggish activity, process or system

juncture- (JUNK-chur) n. a critical point in time; a crisis

junket-n. a pleasure trip; a party, banquet or outing; a trip taken by a public official at public expense; a trip taken by a writer and paid for by a company or government entity

junk science-n. an assortment of biased data, false inferences and logical nonsense that is sometimes presented as courtroom testimony by expert witnesses

j

junta- (HOON-tuh, JUN-tuh) [Spanish] n. a group of military officers ruling a country after seizing power

jury-rig-vb. to assemble for emergency or temporary use; to improvise

juvenescent- (JOO-vuh-NES-unt) adj. becoming young or youthful

juxtapose- (JUKS-tuh-POHZ) vb. to place side by side for comparison or contrast

Kafkaesque-(KAHF-kuh-ESK) adj. nightmarish; confusingly complex

kangaroo court-n. (slang) an illegal, self-appointed court which is characterized by
dishonesty and incompetence

katzenjammer-(KAT-sun-JAM-ur) [German] n. distressing confusion; a loud, harsh
noise; a hangover

k

kef-n. a dreamy, drowsy condition caused by a narcotic; a stupor caused by anything

keister-(KEE-stur) n. (slang) the buttocks; a suitcase

ken-n. the range of knowledge or understanding; perception; an area of authority or expertise

kettle of fish-n. (slang) an embarrassing or difficult situation; a matter to be dealt with

key money-n. money paid by a future tenant to a landlord to assure housing in a market of short supply

keynote-n. the basic idea or principle of a speech, literary work or political platform

keystone-n. a fundamental supporting element

kibitzer-(KIB-its-ur) [Yiddish] n. (slang) a person giving unwanted advice; a busybody

kibosh-(KIH-BAHSH) n. (slang) something that stops something else; a restraint

kickshaw-n. a fancy food or dish; a delicacy

kidvid-n. (slang) television programming for children

killjoy-n. one who destroys or lessens other people's fun or enthusiasm

kingfish-n. (slang) a person holding absolute authority in a group or legislature

kingpin-n. (slang) the most important person or thing in an organization or enterprise

kiosk-(KEE-OSK) n. a small structure used as a newsstand or booth; a small, open pavilion

kismet-(KIZ-met; KIS-mit) n. fate; destiny; lot

kiss and tell-adj. (slang) that which reveals embarrassing or confidential information using firsthand knowledge

kit bag-n. a traveling bag; a knapsack

kitchen cabinet-n. a group of unofficial advisors to the leader of a government

kite-vb. to obtain money or credit by using bad checks; to fraudulently increase the amount of a check

kith-n. a person's friends, neighbors and acquaintances

kitsch-(KICH) [German] n. art or literary works having popular appeal but little artistic merit

kitty-n. money pooled for a specific purpose

knave-(NAYV) n. a dishonest, deceitful person; a male servant

knee-deep-adj. deeply involved or concerned

k

knee-jerk-adj. (slang) easily predictable; automatic

knock-n. (slang) harsh, often petty criticism

kooky-(KOO-kee) adj. (slang) strange; crazy; silly; eccentric

kosher-(KOH-shur) [Yiddish] adj. (slang) authentic; proper; correct

kowtow-(KOU-TOU) vb. to show submissive respect; to brownnose

kudos-(KOO-dahs, -dohz) n. praise or prestige resulting from exceptional achievement

kvetch- (KVECH, kuh-VECH) [Yiddish] vb. (slang) to complain constantly in
  a nagging way; to be insistent

labor of love-n. work performed for personal satisfaction or unselfish reasons rather
    than for financial gain

lackey-n. a male servant of low status; any submissive follower who carries out
    another's orders

lam-n. (slang) escape from the law

1

lame-adj. (slang) ineffective; unconvincing; unsatisfactory; poor; weak

lame duck-n. an elected official who has been defeated for re-election but continues in office until the inauguration of a successor; an ineffective or disabled person

landlubber-n. one unfamiliar with the sea or seamanship

land mine-n. (slang) a hidden, yet beginning crisis

lap dog-n. (slang) a person who wishes to maintain a position of favor or privilege and is eager therefore to fulfill another's wishes

last hurrah-n. a final appearance or effort, as in the end of a career

laundry list-n. (slang) an unorganized list of matters for consideration or things to do; an item-by-item listing

lavender-(LAV-un-dur) adj. light purple

lay of the land-n. the natural features of an area; the existing state of affairs

lazy susan-n. a revolving tray containing food or seasonings

leap frog-vb. to move or progress in stages

leaseback-n. a business transaction whereby property is simultaneously sold and leased back to the seller for long-term continued use

legal eagle-n. (slang) a highly-skilled, clever lawyer

legalese-(LEE-guh-LEEZ, -LEES) n. the specialized vocabulary of the legal profession, often considered incomprehensible to the layman

legerdemain-(LEJ-ur-duh-MAIN) n. magic tricks; sleight of hand; deceitful cleverness

legman-n. (slang) a news reporter who gathers information at the scene of events; an office assistant who runs errands or does routine tasks

leitmotif-(LITE-moh-TEEF) [German] n. a dominant, recurring theme, as in a novel or musical composition

lethologica-(LETH-all-OH-jih-kuh) n. a momentary inability to remember a name or a word

letter of credit-n. a letter from a bank authorizing the holder to draw a specified amount of money from the issuing bank, its branches or other associated banks

leveraged buyout-n. the purchase of a corporation by investors using borrowed funds which are secured by the assets of the acquired corporation

leviathan- (luh-VIE-uh-thun) adj. something enormous or very powerful

lickety-split-adv. (slang) with great speed

lifeblood-n. a vital element or force; anything indispensable to existence

lifer-n. (slang) a person who spends an entire working career in a certain occupation; a prisoner serving a life sentence; one who makes a career in the armed forces

light-fingered-adj. skilled at picking pockets

lightning rod-n. a person who attracts and causes negative feelings and reactions in order to shift interest from other issues

lilliputian-(LIL-uh-PYOO-shun) adj. tiny; narrow-minded; petty

lily-livered-(LIV-urd) adj. cowardly; shy

limerick-(LIM-ur-ik, LIM-rik) n. a humorous poem of five lines

linchpin-n. the main unifying element; the crucial element in an organization or argument

lionize-vb. to regard or treat as a celebrity

lip service-n. an insincere expression of loyalty, respect or support

literati-(LIT-uh-RAH-tee) [Latin] n. scholars; distinguished writers

litmus test-n. a test in which a single factor determines the result

liverish-(LIV-ur-ish) adj. irritable; grouchy; disagreeable

lobster shift-n. (slang) the night shift of any work force

loco-(LOH-koh) [Spanish] adj. (slang) crazy; insane

logjam-n. a deadlock in negotiations

logorrhea-(LOG-uh-REE-uh) n. excessive, uncontrollable talkativeness

lollapalooza-(LALL-uh-puh-LOO-zuh) n. (slang) someone or something very exceptional, outstanding or striking. Also lollapaloosa.

lollygag-vb. (slang) fool around; to waste time in a purposeless activity

longhair-n. (slang) a classical music enthusiast; a domestic cat that has long fur

long suit-n. a talent or quality that is one's strongest asset

looby-n. a big, clumsy person

loop-n. within the sphere of influence or activity

loopy-adj. (slang) crazy; foolish; offbeat; confused due to intoxication

loose cannon-n. (slang) an uncontrollable person who poses danger

lope-vb. to run or gallop at an easy, steady pace

loss leader-n. any article that a store sells at or below cost to attract customers

louche-(LOOSH) [French] adj. shady; questionable

1

lounge lizard-n. (slang) a pleasure-seeking person frequenting nightclubs where the wealthy socialize

lout-n. an awkward, stupid person

love affair-n. a strong enthusiasm

love feast-n. any gathering marked by good feeling and friendliness

low-ball-vb. (slang) to understate a cost deliberately without intending to honor it

lowbrow-n. (slang) a person lacking refinement

lowest common denominator-n. that which is accepted or understood by a majority of people

lubber-n. a big, clumsy person

lucre-(LOO-kur) [Latin] n. money; riches

luft mensch-(LOOFT MENSH) [German] n. an impractical, unrealistic person

luminary-(LOO-muh-NAIR-ee) n. a celebrity; a famous intellectual; a person who inspires or enlightens mankind

lumpish-adj. stupid; dull; clumsy

lunatic fringe-(LOO-nuh-tik) n. the extremist, fanatical or irrational members of a group or society

luteous-(LOO-tee-us) adj. light greenish-yellow

lyncean-(lin-SEE-un) adj. sharp-sighted; eagle-eyed

lysophobia-(LIE-soh-FOH-bee-uh) n. an obsessive fear of going insane. Also lyssophobia.

macabre- (muh-KAH-bruh, muh-KAHB-) adj. horrifying; gruesome

Machiavellian- (MAK-ee-uh-VEL-ee-un) adj. crafty; deceitful; cunning; scheming

machination- (MAK-uh-NAY-shun) n. a crafty plot or scheme, usually with evil intent; a conspiracy

madcap-adj. reckless; wild; impulsive

maelstrom- (MAIL-strum) n. a large or violent whirlpool; a violent or turbulent situation

magenta- (muh-JEN-tuh) adj. purplish-red

magic bullet-n. (slang) a drug or therapy that cures or prevents a disease; something held as a magical solution to a serious problem or a means of avoiding a disaster

magnate- (MAG-NATE, -nit) n. a very rich, powerful and influential person in business

magniloquent- (mag-NIL-uh-kwunt) adj. boastful or high-sounding in speech or style; bragging

maize- (MAYZ) n. corn; deep yellow

makeover-n. an overall treatment to change an image or improve an appearance

makeshift-adj. suitable as a temporary, advantageous or convenient substitute

maladroit- (MAL-uh-DROIT) adj. awkward; clumsy; unskilled

malaise- (muh-LAYZ) n. a feeling of unease or distress; a general sense of economic, moral or social decline

malapropism- (MAL-uh-PROP-iz-um) n. a humorous or ridiculous misuse of a word caused by a resemblance in sound, as in "ideals" for "ideas"

malcontent-n. a dissatisfied, rebellious person, especially one unhappy with the
government or an economic system

malleable- (MAL-ee-uh-bul) adj. easy to bend or shape; adaptable; easily controlled
or influenced

mangy- (MAIN-jee) adj. rundown and filthy; shabby; mean and lowdown

mammalucco- (MAH-mah-LUKE-oh) [Italian] n. (slang) a fool; a nitwit

maniacal- (muh-NIE-uh-kul) adj. raving mad; wildly insane; characterized by
extreme excitement or enthusiasm

manifesto- (MAN-uh-FES-toh) [Italian] n. a public declaration of political beliefs,
policies and principles

manna-n. something desperately needed that comes unexpectedly

mantra- (MAHN-truh) n. a chant of words or syllables

mare's-nest-n. a hoax or fraud; a delusion; an extremely complicated situation

marginalize-vb. to ignore or exclude by confining to a lower or outer limit

marked-adj. noticeable; obvious; clearly evident

maroon- (muh-ROON) vb. to abandon; to leave helpless or isolated

marshal-vb. to arrange in order; to gather and organize

martinet- (MAR-tih-NET) n. a strict military disciplinarian; any strict disciplinarian who adheres to rigid regulations

masher-n. (slang) a man who makes unwanted advances toward women

masterstroke-n. a decisive action or achievement; a stroke of genius

material-adj. important; significant; substantial

matted-adj. tangled in a dense mass

matutinal- (muh-TOOT-ih-nul) adj. relating to or happening in the morning; early

maudlin-adj. foolishly and tearfully sentimental; overly emotional

maunder-vb. to talk or walk in an aimless, confused manner

maven- (MAY-vun) n. (slang) an expert having special experience or knowledge in a particular field or activity. Also mavin.

maverick- (MAV-ur-ik, MAV-rik) n. a rebel; a nonconformist; a dissenter

mawkish-adj. overly emotional; sentimental; misty-eyed; dull; tasteless

maxim-n. a briefly stated rule of conduct or general truth that is frequently quoted

mayday-n. the international radiotelephone signal word for "help" that is used by aircraft and ships in distress

maze-n. a complex, confusing network of winding pathways; anything consisting of many conflicting, confused elements

meal ticket-n. (slang) a person, job, skill or thing relied on as a source of financial support

mealy-adj. crumbled; granular; pale; spotted

mealy-mouthed-adj. unwilling to state facts or opinions directly and simply; evasive

means testing-n. a controversial proposal, as applied to benefits such as Social Security and Medicare, to calculate a recipient's benefits on income rather than the number of years worked or the amount paid in overtime

meatball-n. (slang) a stupid, clumsy or boring person

meddlesome-adj. interfering; overcurious; snooping

media circus-n. sensationalized, overkill coverage of an apparently newsworthy event by the news media

megalopolis- (MEG-uh-LOP-uh-lis) n. an extensive, heavily-populated urban region that includes a number of cities

megrims- (MEE-grims) n. depression; unhappiness

mélange- (may-LAHNG, -LAHNZH) [French] n. a mixture; a medley

melee- (MAY-lay) [French] n. a brawl; a violent free-for-all; noisy confusion

mellifluous- (muh-LIF-loo-us) adj. flowing or sounding sweet and smooth

meltdown-n. extreme overheating of a nuclear reactor core leading to the escape of radiation and melting of the core; a decline and breakdown in a situation

ménage- (may-NAHZH, muh-) [French] n. a household; housekeeping

menagerie- (muh-NAJ-uh-ee, muh-NAZH-uh-ree) [French] n. a collection of wild or odd-looking animals on exhibition

mendacious- (men-DAY-shus) adj. dishonest; lying

mensch- (MENSCH) [Yiddish] n. (slang) a person having the qualities of wisdom, honor, maturity and responsibility

menticide- (MEN-tih-SIDE) n. brainwashing; the destruction of a mind

mercantile- (MUR-kun-TEEL) adj. relating to business, trade or merchants; commercial

mercenary- (MUR-suh-NAIR-ee) n. a hired soldier; a person who will do anything for money

mercurial- (mur-KYOOR-ee-ul) adj. having sudden, unpredictable mood changes; shrewd; quick-witted; lively

meretricious- (MAIR-uh-TRISH-us) adj. acting flashy to attract attention; believable but false or insincere; relating to prostitutes

meritocracy- (MAIR-ih-TOK-ruh-see) n. a system in which promotion is based on individual achievement or ability

mestizo- (mes-TEE-zoh) [Spanish] n. a person of mixed racial ancestry

metage- (MEET-ij) n. an official measurement of the weight of commodities such as coal and grain

metamorphosis- (MET-uh-MOR-fuh-sis) n. a striking or sudden change in appearance, condition or function; a magical change in form

mete- (MEET) [French] vb. to allocate; to distribute; to apportion

meteoric- (MEET-ee-OR-ik) adj. momentarily swift, flashing or brilliant

metonymy- (muh-TAHN-uh-mee) n. a figure of speech in which one word or phrase is substituted for another closely associated with it, as in the "White House" for the "presidency"

mettle-n. courage; vigorous energy; quality of character and temperament

miasma- (mie-AZ-muh, mee-AZ-MUH) n. an odor of decaying matter; a harmful influence or atmosphere; a confusing subject or event

Mickey Mouse-n. (slang) annoyingly petty; over-simplified; thrown together
haphazardly; childish

microbrewery-n. a small brewery, commonly in a specialized restaurant where the
product, beer, is sold

micromanage-vb. to become overly concerned or involved with the work of
lower-level managers

micro-marketing-n. a new form of niche marketing whereby larger markets are
studied and smaller, more clearly defined markets targeted, such as over-40
easy-listening music fans

mien- (MEEN) n. an appearance, manner or bearing which reveals one's character
or attitude

miffed-adj. annoyed; upset; offended

milestone-n. an important event in a person's career or a nation's history;
developments in a particular field; a turning point

milieu- (mil-YOO) [French] n. an environment or setting surrounding a person
or thing

militant- (MIL-ih-tunt) adj. fighting; combative; being aggressive in supporting
a specific cause

militate-(MIL-ih-TATE) vb. to have an influence or effect on

milk-livered- (LIV-urd) adj. cowardly; timid

milk run-n. (slang) a routine trip having many stops

millstone-n. a heavy burden or weight

milquetoast- (MILK-TOAST) [French] n. a shy, meek, apologetic individual

minacious- (mih-NAY-shus) adj. threatening; unfavorable; menacing

mincing-adj. dainty; delicate; refined

mind-set-n. a fixed mental attitude or disposition created by one's education, experience or prejudices; a habit; a tendency

mind's eye-n. one's imagination or memory

mingy- (MIN-jee) adj. (slang) mean and stingy; of small quantity

minimalist-n. a person who advocates a conservative policy or action, as in a political or governmental organization

minion- (MIN-yun) n. an overflattering follower of an important or powerful individual; a yes man

ministerial- (MIN-ih-STEER-ee-ul) adj. relating to the administrative functions of government; functioning as an agent; instrumental

minutiae- (mih-NOO-shuh) n. small, petty or insignificant details

minx- n. a young, flirtatious, sexy woman

mirabile dictu- (MEER-ah-bee-lay DIK-TOO) [Latin] interj. wonderful to tell

misanthrope- (MIS-un-THROHP) n. one who hates or mistrusts all people

miscreant- (MIS-kree-unt) adj. an evil person; a villain

misogamy- (mih-SOG-uh-mee) n. a hatred of marriage

misogyny- (mih-SOJ-uh-nee) n. a hatred of women

misology- (mih-SALL-uh-jee) n. a hatred of reasoning, argument, debate or enlightenment

misoneism- (MIS-oh-NEE-IZ-um) n. a hatred or fear of change or innovation

misopedia- (MIS-oh-PEE-DEE-uh) n. a hatred of children

missive- (MIS-iv) n. a letter; a written message

mixed bag-n. a mixture or collection of various objects, elements or people

mixed grill-n. a meal made of various broiled meats and vegetables

mixologist- (miks-ALL-uh-jist) n. (slang) a bartender

mnemonic- (nih-MAHN-ik) adj. assisting or intending to help the memory

mock-up-n. a full-sized model of a structure used for experimental or instructional purposes

modicum- (MOD-ih-kum) n. a small amount; a limited quantity

modish- (MOH-dish) adj. fashionable; trendy; current

modus operandi- (MOH-dus OP-uh-RAN-dee, -die) [Latin] n. a method of operating or doing something

mogul- (MOH-GUL) n. a very rich, powerful or influential person; a small mound or bump of tightly packed snow on a ski slope

moiety- (MOY-ih-tee) n. a half; a portion or share

moil-n. hard work; toil; confusion; turmoil

mojo- (MOH-joh) n. a charm or trinket that is thought to have magical powers

mole-n. (slang) a spy who operates within an enemy's government or intelligence agency; a double agent who operates against one's own government from within its intelligence organization

mollycoddle-vb. to pamper; to be overprotective; to cater to

monger- (MAHN-gur, MUNG-) n. a person promoting something undesirable; a dealer or trader in specific goods

moniker- (MAHN-ih-kur) n. (slang) a person's name or nickname

monkeyshine-n. (slang) a playful joke or trick; a prank

monkey suit-n. (slang) a man's dress suit; a uniform

monkey wrench-n. (slang) something disrupting

Montessori method- (MAHN-tih-SOR-ee) n. a system of educating young children which emphasizes developing a pupil's own natural abilities and motivation

moonstruck-adj. romantically dreamy or obsessed; crazed; insane

morass- (muh-RASS) n. a swamp or marsh; something that overwhelms, confuses or hinders

mordant- (MOR-dunt) adj. sarcastic; biting; cutting; incisive

morning after-n. (slang) a hangover; a painful awakening

morose- (muh-ROHS) adj. gloomy; grim; sad; dejected

Moses-n. a political candidate perceived to be figuratively "roaming the desert" of the talk-show circuit instead of focusing on specific issues

most-favored nation-n. a nation given privileges of trade under a government policy if certain conditions are met

mothball-vb. to postpone indefinitely; to shelve; to put in storage

motif- (moh-TEEF) [French] n. a recurring idea or theme in an artistic or literary work; a repeated design in architecture or decoration; a central idea or theme

motley- (MOT-lee) adj. composed of many different elements; multi-colored

moulage- (moo-LAHZH) [French] n. a mold of a footprint or object made for use in a criminal investigation

mountebank- (MOUN-tuh-BANK) n. a flamboyant impostor or quack; a boastful pretender

mousemilking-n. (slang) the investment of maximum time and effort for minimum return, as on a business venture or an academic project

mousy-adj. quiet; shy; having a dull brownish color; having small, sharp features

mouthpiece-n. (slang) a spokesperson through which views are expressed; a criminal defense lawyer

mover and shaker-n. a person possessing power and influence within a particular field of endeavor

moxie- (MOK-see) n. (slang) courage; aggressive energy; initiative; common sense
and know how; perseverance

mucid- (MYOO-sid) adj. musty; moldy

muck-n. anything unclean or degrading; filth

muck-a-muck-n. (slang) an important, high-ranking individual who is
often overbearing

muckrake-vb. to investigate and report in the media the corruption and misconduct
of public officials and business executives

mufti- (MUF-tee) n. ordinary clothes worn by a person who usually wears a uniform;
civilian clothing

mugwump- (MUG-WUMP) n. a person who remains neutral on political or other
issues; one who acts independently

muliebrity- (MYOO-lee-EB-rih-tee) n. womanhood; femininity

mulligrubs-n. intestinal pain or discomfort

multiplex- (MUL-tuh-PLEKS) n. a building, such as a movie theater or residence,
containing separate units

mum-adj. silent; not speaking

mumbo jumbo-n. confusing and complicated language or activity

mummery- (MUM-uh-ree) n. a ridiculous, overdone ceremony or performance;
    farce; burlesque

munchkin-n. (slang) a child; a small person with an elf-like appearance

muse-vb. to meditate; to ponder; to be absorbed in one's thoughts

mushroom-vb. grow, multiply or spread rapidly

myopia- (mie-OH-pee-uh) n. nearsightedness; a lack of foresight in thinking
    or planning

myriad- (MIR-ee-ud) n. a very large, indefinite number
    adj. countless; having a varied nature

mythos- (MIE-thos, MITH-os) [Greek] n. a myth or mythology; the basic attitudes,
    beliefs and values of a particular group or society

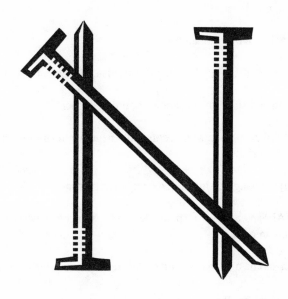

nabob- (NAY-bob) n. a wealthy, prominent person

nag-n. (slang) a racehorse; an old, worn-out horse

namby-pamby-adj. wishy-washy; indecisive; lacking vigor; exhibiting weak
    sentimentality

n

namesake-n. one who is named after another

narly-adj. difficult; problematic

nary- (NAIR-ee) adj. not one; not any

nascence- (NAY-sense) n. the origin of a concept, idea, movement or organization

natty-adj. neat, trim and smart in appearance or dress; dapper

naysayer- (NAY-SAY-ur) n. one who is outwardly negative in attitude; one who critically disagrees

nebbish- [Yiddish] n. (slang) a shy, dull, incompetent person

ne'er-do-well- (NAIR) n. a lazy, irresponsible person; someone who is ineffective and lacking in merit

nemesis- (NEM-ih-sis) n. a source of ruin or danger; an unbeatable opponent or rival

neo- [Greek] pref. new; recent; new and different

neologism- (nee-ALL-uh-JIZ-um) n. a new word, expression or meaning for an existing word

nerve center-n. a control center; a headquarters; a source of power or influence

nettlesome-adj. irritating; annoying; disturbing

networking-n. an informal exchange of information or development of contacts among individuals having common interests or concerns, especially in regard to furthering a career

newfangled- (NOO-FANG-guld) adj. new; novel

newspeak-n. deliberately unclear, contradictory language used to control or influence public opinion

New World Order-n. collective security and other interests among formerly mutually hostile nations

nexus- (NEK-sus) n. a means of connection; a link or tie; the center or core

niggle-vb. to waste time by preoccupation with petty details; to criticize constantly about trivial matters

niminy-piminy-adj. fussily delicate or refined

nine days' wonder-n. anything that generates brief excitement or interest

nitpick-vb. to pay too much attention to or find fault with insignificant details

nix-n. (slang) nothing
vb. to forbid; to refuse

no-holds-barred-adj. (slang) open and unrestrained

no man's land-n. an area of uncertainty or confusion; an unclaimed or unowned piece of land

nom de plume- (NOM-duh-PLOOM) [French] n. a pen name

nondescript-adj. lacking distinctive qualities or form; difficult to classify or describe; uninteresting

nonesuch-n. someone or something unequalled or unique

non grata- (non GRAH-tuh, GRAT-uh) [Latin] adj. not approved; unwelcome

nonpareil- (NON-puh-rel) [French] adj. unequaled; unrivaled

nonplused-adj. confused; puzzled; baffled

non sequitur- (non SEK-wih-tur) [Latin] n. a conclusion or inference that does not follow from the evidence or premises; a statement that does not follow logically from what preceded it

noodge- (NOOJ) [Yiddish] vb. (slang) to keep asking or urging in an annoying way; to nag

nosh- [Yiddish] n. (slang) a snack or light meal

nouveau riche- (NOO-voh REESH) [French] n. one who has recently become rich and commonly displays the newly acquired wealth

nouvelle cuisine- (noo-VEL kwih-ZEEN) [French] n. a modern style of French cooking that emphasizes the use of natural ingredients and light sauces with low fat and starch

nub-n. (slang) the essence; the gist of a matter

nuclear family-n. the basic family unit consisting of parents and their children living in one household

nudnick- (NOOD-nik) [Yiddish] n. (slang) a tiresome; annoying person; a pest

number cruncher-n. (slang) a person or computer capable of performing lengthy, complex calculations swiftly

nursemaid-n. a woman employed to care for children

nut case-n. (slang) a crazy or eccentric person

obloquy- (OB-luh-kwee) n. dishonor or disgrace resulting from abusive or
        defamatory language; damage to one's reputation

obumbrate- (uh-BUM-brate) vb. to make difficult to see or understand

odd man out-n. a person of unconventional behavior or beliefs

odds-on-adj. (slang) having an excellent chance of success; more likely than others to win

offbeat-n. (slang) unconventional; unusual; atypical

officious- (uh-FISH-us) adj. annoyingly eager to offer unwanted advice or services to others; overbearing; interfering

offish-adj. distant and reserved in manner; aloof

off-key-adj. not in accord with what is considered normal or appropriate

offshoot-n. anything that develops or branches out from a particular source

off-the-cuff-adj., adv. without preparation; spur-of-the-moment

off-the-record-adj., adv. not for publication

off-the-shelf-adj. merchandise that is available for purchase without modification

old-boy network-n. an informal system of mutual friendship and assistance through which men belonging to a particular group exchange favors and contacts, as in business or politics

oldfangled- (OLD-FANG-uld) adj. old-fashioned

old guard-n. a conservative, often reactionary element of a group, society or political party; a group that has long defended a particular cause

old hat-adj. (slang) old-fashioned; outdated; overused

oligarchy- (ALL-ih-GAR-kee, OH-lih-) n. a government in which a small group exercises ruling power

olio- (OH-lee-OH) n. a mixture or medley of various elements; a collection of various musical, literary or artistic works

olive branch-n. any offer of peace

ombudsman- (OM-budz-mun, AHM-boodz-) n. an official who investigates complaints made by private citizens against the government, institutions, corporations or organizations and mediates settlements for those involved

omnibus- (OM-nih-bus) [Latin] adj. including or providing for many items at once; having a variety of uses or purposes

omnifarious- (OM-nih-FAIR-ee-us) adj. of all varieties or forms; diverse

once-over-n. (slang) a quick, thorough glance, inspection or survey

oniomania- (ON-ee-oh-MAIN-ee-uh) n. an uncontrolled urge to buy things

onomatopoeia- (ON-uh-MAHT-oh-PEE-uh) [Latin] n. the formation of words that imitate natural sounds as in "buzz" or "hiss"

onus- (OH-nus) n. a burden; an obligation; blame; the burden of proof

op-ed page-n. a newspaper section, usually opposite the editorial page, that features articles, columns and letters expressing various personal opinions and observations

open adoption-n. an arrangement whereby the adoptive and biological parents maintain contact between each other in the adoption process

open-and-shut-adj. (slang) easily determined; obvious

open door-n. free access; an unrestricted opportunity

operative- (OP-ur-uh-tiv) n. a spy; a private detective; a skilled industrial worker

opine- (oh-PINE) vb. to hold or express an opinion

oppugn- (uh-PYOON) vb. to oppose; to attack; to criticize; to disagree

opt out-vb. (slang) to choose not to participate in something

organization man-n. an employee of a large corporation who has lost a sense of personal independence or identity because of adapting so completely to what is expected by the corporation

orphan drug-n. a pharmaceutical product that is used to treat diseases that infect relatively few patients and is thus less profitable to manufacture

oscitant- (OS-ih-tunt) adj. lazy; inattentive; drowsy

osculate- (OS-kyuh-LATE) vb. to kiss; to hug; to touch closely

osmosis- (os-MOH-sis) n. a gradual, often unconscious process of attaining something through exposure to it

otiose- (OH-tee-OHS, OH-shee-) adj. lazy; useless; ineffective

outdistance-vb. to surpass completely through superior skill or endurance

outlander-n. a foreigner; a stranger; an outsider

outré- (oo-TRAY) [French] adj. bizarre; eccentric; exaggerated

outrider-n. a trailblazer; a forerunner; a guide; an escort

outsourcing-n. arrangements made by the government and large corporations to assign some specialized services, such as security and data processing, to private industry

outtake-n. a scene or section of a movie or television program that is not included in the final version

overdub-vb. to add sounds or music to a previously taped musical recording to heighten the total effect

over-the-top-adj. (slang) outrageous; being extreme in character

overture-n. an act, offer or proposal intended to initiate negotiations or a
relationship; an introductory, instrumental composition to an extended work,
as in an opera

oxymoron- (OK-see-MOR-ON) n. a figure of speech in which opposite ideas or
terms are combined, as in "sweet sorrow" or "deafening silence"

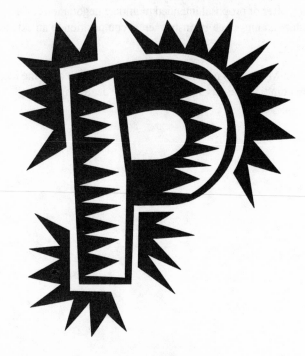

pablum- n. dull or simplistic writing, speech or ideas

pack rat- n. (slang) one who saves or hoards numerous items, many of which
      may be useless

paisano- (pie-ZAH-noh) [Italian] n. (slang) a friend or pal; a fellow countryman

p

paladin- (PAL-uh-din) n. a knight; a heroic champion; a strong defender or supporter of a cause

palatable- (PAL-uh-tuh-bul) adj. pleasing to the taste; agreeable to the mind or feelings

palaver- (puh-LAV-ur) n. meaningless chatter; flattery

palindrome- (PAL-in-DROME) n. a word, phrase or sentence, such as "madam" or "radar" that reads the same backward or forward

palindromia- (PAL-in-DROH-mee-uh) n. the recurrence of a disease

palliate- (PAL-ee-ATE) vb. to lessen or relieve without eliminating the problem; to ease pain; to make appear less offensive or serious

pallid- (PAL-id) adj. pale; dull; uninteresting

palooka- (puh-LOO-kuh) n. (slang) a clumsy or stupid person; an incompetent athlete

palpable- (PAL-puh-bul) adj. touchable; able to be understood readily by the mind or senses; obvious

palsy-walsy- adj. (slang) very friendly

pan-vb. (slang) to criticize or review harshly; to rotate a television or movie camera horizontally to follow an object or create a comprehensive effect

panacea- (PAN-uh-SEE-uh) n. a cure or remedy for all ills, diseases, evils or difficulties; a cure-all

panache- (puh-NASH, -NOSH) [French] n. flamboyance; spirited self-assurance; elegance of manner or sophistication

pandemic- (pan-DEM-ik) adj. universal; widespread; affecting a majority of people as in a disease

pander-vb. to appeal to the lower desires or tastes of someone; to exploit the needs and weaknesses of others

panegyric- (PAN-uh-JEER-ik, -JIE-rik) n. high praise or tribute of a person or event; a formal speech or writing that expresses such

panjandrum- (pan-JAN-drum) n. a self-important, boasting individual

panoply- (PAN-uh-plee) n. any impressive, magnificent display or group

pap-n. (slang) writings or ideas lacking real substance or value; money and favors received because of identification with public office

paparazzi- (PAH-puh-ROTS-zee) [Italian] n. photographers who aggressively pursue celebrities in order to take pictures for sale to newspapers and magazines

paperhanger-n. (slang) a person who passes bad checks or counterfeit paper money

p

paper tiger-n. a person or nation that is perceived to be dangerous and powerful but is actually weak, ineffective or shy

paper trail-n. (slang) documented evidence of one's actions

paradigm- (PAR-uh-DIME, -DIM) n. an example that serves as a model or pattern; a standard to hold up for comparison

paralogism- (puh-RAL-uh-JIZ-um) n. an illogical argument or conclusion drawn from a series of facts

paramilitary-adj. being or relating to civilians who are organized to assist or operate in place of a regular military organization; having a military structure

paramour- (PAIR-uh-MOOR) [Latin] n. the lover or mistress of a married person

pare-vb. to remove the skin or outer covering of; to peel; to reduce; to diminish

parenthetical- (PAIR-un-THET-ih-kul) adj. explanatory; qualifying; containing or using parentheses

par excellence- (EK-suh-LAHNS) [French] adj. being the best of a kind; beyond comparison

pariah- (puh-RIE-uh) n. a social outcast; a person despised or rejected by others

parlance- (PAR-luns) n. a style or manner of speaking or writing

parlay- (PAR-lay, -lee) vb. to bet an original wager and its winnings on another contest or race; to utilize or exploit successfully

parley- (PAR-LAY, -lee) n. a conference or discussion to settle a specific dispute or examine a specific matter

parlous- (PAR-lus) adj. dangerous; hazardous; clever; shrewd

parochial- (puh-ROH-kee-ul) adj. very narrow in outlook, point of view or scope

parody- (PAIR-uh-dee) n. a literary or musical work that is a humorous imitation; an intentional mockery

paroxysm- (PAR-uk-SIZ-um) n. a sudden fit or outburst of pain, rage or laughter; a sudden, severe recurrence of the symptoms of a disease

parsimonious- (PAR-suh-MOH-nee-us) adj. stingy; very thrifty; penny-pinching

partisan- (PAR-tih-zun) adj. one-sided; committed to a party, person, cause or idea

parvenu- (PAR-vuh-NOO) [French] n. a person who has recently acquired money or social status but has not yet gained social acceptance by others in that class

pash-n. (slang) a strong romantic infatuation or affection

passé- (PAS-AY) [French] adj. old-fashioned; out-of-date; aged; faded

pass muster-vb. to measure up to a given standard; to pass an inspection or examination

p

pastel- (pas-TEL) n. a soft, delicate shade of any color

pastiche- (pas-TEESH, pahs-) [French] n. a literary, dramatic or musical work composed of a combination of borrowed styles or themes; a mixture of various items

pastoral- (PAS-tur-ul) adj. relating to country life; rural; peaceful; calm; restful

pat-adj. timely; suitable; so smoothly and easily communicated as to seem contrived

patchwork-n. anything formed with odd, miscellaneous parts; a quilt or other needlework consisting of various patches of cloth sewn together

pathetic fallacy-n. a linking of human emotions and characteristics to nature and inactive objects, as in the "angry sea" or the "cruel wind"

pathos- (PAY-THOS, -THAHS) [Greek] n. tender sorrow; pity; sympathy; the quality in something experienced or observed that produces such feelings

patois- (puh-TWAH) [French] n. a local dialect spoken by people of a certain area that is distinct from the standard language; jargon of a particular group

patrician- (puh-TRISH-un) n. a person of high social standing or refinement; an aristocrat

patsy- n. (slang) one easily blamed, cheated, taken advantage of or ridiculed

patter-n. chatter; meaningless talk; rapid, smooth speech, as of a comedian
 or auctioneer

peccadillo- (PEK-uh-DIL-oh) [Latin] n. a minor offense or fault; a small sin

pecking order-n. a social organization based on income, status or authority;
 a hierarchy of relationships and power

pecuniary- (pih-KYOO-nee-AIR-ee) adj. relating to or involving money; financial;
 requiring payment of money

pedagogue- (PED-uh-GOG) n. an overly strict, narrow-minded schoolteacher
 or educator

pedantic- (puh-DAN-tik) adj. intellectually showing off or boring; overly concerned
 with minor details or formal rules

pedestrian- (puh-DES-TREE-un) adj. ordinary; unimaginative; dull

pedigree- (PED-ih-GREE) n. a list or line of ancestors; a source; background

peevish-adj. irritable; ill-tempered; hard to please

pejorative- (pih-JOR-uh-tiv) adj. negative; demeaning; tending to become or
 make worse

pelagic- (puh-LAJ-ik) adj. pertaining to the open seas or oceans

p

pell-mell-n. disorder; turmoil; confusion
   adv. recklessly; helter-skelter; abruptly

pellucid- (puh-LOO-sid) adj. admitting the passage of light; clear and simple in
   style or meaning; easy to understand

penchant- (PEN-chunt) n. a strong liking or fondness for something; a taste;
   a tendency

pending-adj. awaiting conclusion; not yet decided or settled; close at hand

penny ante-adj. (slang) an insignificant undertaking or business proposal

pensive-adj. thoughtful and sad; showing deep, dreamy thoughtfulness

pent-up-adj. not given expression; held in

penultimate- (pih-NUL-tuh-mut) adj. next to last

perchance-adj. perhaps; possibly; accidentally

percipient- (pur-SIP-ee-unt) adj. perceiving or comprehending keenly and readily

percolate- (PUR-kuh-LATE) vb. to drip or pass through; to strain; to brew;
   to become active or lively

peregrination- (PAIR-ih-gruh-NAY-shun) n. a journey or expedition without
   particular plans

peremptory (pur-EMP-tuh-ree, puh-REMP-) adj. absolute; final; leaving no room for argument or rebuttal; excessively self-confident

perfunctory- (pur-FUNK-tuh-ree) adj. unenthusiastic; indifferent; without concern; routine; not thorough; careless

peripatetic- (PAIR-uh-puh-TET-ik) adj. wandering or traveling from place to place

peripheral- (puh-RIF-ur-ul) adj. outlying; outer; unimportant; not relevant

per se- (pur-SAY) [Latin] adv. in or by itself; by definition

persiflage- (PIR-sih-FLAHZH) n. light, good-natured speech or writing; a light treatment or discussion of a subject

persnickety- (pur-SNIK-ih-tee) adj. (slang) overattentive to minor details; overdemanding; fussy

persona- (pur-SOH-nuh) [Latin] n. one's personality or public image; the characters in a literary or dramatic work

persona non grata- (non GRAH-tuh, -GRAT-uh) [Latin] n. a person who is not welcomed or acceptable

perspicacious- (PUR-spih-KAY-shus) adj. having insight; having keen judgment or understanding; perceptive; shrewd

perspicuous- (pur-SPIK-yoo-us) adj. clearly expressed; easily understood

P

pert-adj. bold or forward in behavior or speech; stylish in appearance; high-spirited; lively

pertinacious- (PUR-tuh-NAY-shus) adj. stubborn; unyielding; persistent

peruse- (puh-ROOZ) vb. to read or study carefully; to examine

pesky-adj. (slang) annoying; troublesome; irritating

Peter Principle-n. the theory that each employee in an organization will advance until reaching his or her level of incompetence

pettifogger- (PET-ih-FOG-ur) n. a dishonest lawyer who uses unethical methods and handles trumped-up cases; a person overly concerned with minor details

petulant- (PECH-uh-lunt) adj. cranky; rude; impatient or irritable over a minor annoyance; touchy

pharisaic (FAR-ih-SAY-ik) adj. pretending to be virtuous without actually being so; resembling self-righteous hypocrisy

phatic- (FAT-ik) adj. relating to speech used merely to establish friendship or sociability rather than to communicate ideas or information

Philadelphia lawyer-n. (slang) a clever, shrewd attorney who is skilled in discovering and taking advantage of legal technicalities

philander- (Fih-LAN-dur) vb. to engage in many insincere, passing love affairs; to flirt

philippic- (Fih-LIP-ik) n. a speech that bitterly attacks a person or thing

philistine- (FIL-ih-steen) n. an uncultured, narrow-minded person

philobat- (FIL-oh-bat) n. a lover of travel

phlegmatic- (fleg-MAT-ik) adj. calm; unemotional; indifferent

phrenic- (FREN-ik) adj. relating to the mind; mental

picaresque- (PIK-uh-RESK) adj. involving clever villains or adventurers

picayune- (PIK-uh-YOON) adj. petty; trivial; minor; small

pickled-adj. (slang) drunk; intoxicated

piebald-adj. irregularly spotted or patched in two colors

piece-n. an artistic, literary or musical work; a firearm

piéce de résistance- (pees duh ray-zee-STAHNS) [French] n. an outstanding achievement; the main dish of a meal

piecemeal-adj., adv. piece by piece; into pieces or parts; gradually

pied piper-n. one who offers others tempting yet misleading hopes or promises

pie-eyed-adj. (slang) intoxicated; drunk

p

pie-in-the-sky-n. (slang) an empty, unrealistic promise or wish; a promise of a reward or benefits in the distant future

piffle-n., interj. foolish talk or ideas; nonsense;

pigeonhole-vb. to categorize; to classify; to put aside indefinitely as to ignore or forget

piker-n. (slang) an overly cautious gambler or speculator; a stingy or petty individual

pill-n. (slang) a boring or unpleasant person

pillory- (PIL-uh-ree) n. an exposure to public contempt or scorn

pink-collar-adj. pertaining to a class of jobs traditionally filled by women, as in clerical or secretarial positions

pipe dream-n. (slang) an unrealistic hope or plan; a fantastic idea

piquant- (PEE-kunt, pee-KAHNT) adj. spicy or pleasantly sharp in taste; fascinating; stimulating

pique- (PEEK) vb. to annoy; to irritate; to humiliate; to stimulate; to excite

pissant-n. (slang) a person overly concerned with petty details

pit-bull-adj. (slang) characterized by or showing extreme aggression, ruthlessness or bitterness

pitchman-n. (slang) any high-pressure salesman; a person who delivers commercials on radio or TV; a seller of small articles at a carnival or on a city street

pithy-adj. meaningful; profound; brief and forceful

pivotal- (PIV-uh-tul) adj. crucial; key; of vital importance

placate- (PLAY-KATE) vb. to calm; to soothe; to please; to relieve

placebo- (pluh-SEE-boh) n. a harmless substance without healing properties that is given to satisfy a patient; a harmless substance used as a control in experimental tests to check the effectiveness of a drug; something that is said or done to reassure another

plaintive- (PLAIN-tiv) adj. sorrowful; sad; mournful

plank-n. any article or principle of a political platform

platitude- (PLAT-ih-TOOD) n. a commonplace, dull or empty statement that is usually expressed as being original, important or profound

platonic- (pluh-TAHN-ik, play-) adj. purely spiritual; idealistic; nonsexual

plaudit- (PLAW-dit) n. an expression of praise or approval

plausible- (PLAW-zuh-bul) adj. apparently believable or true

player-n. an active participant in an activity or endeavor

p

plebeian- (plih-BEE-un) adj. common; ordinary; unrefined; unpolished

plenary- (PLEN-uh-ree, PLEE-nuh-) adj. full; complete; absolute

plenipotentiary- (PLEN-uh-puh-TEN-shee-AIR-ee, -shuh-ree) n. a person given full authority to act on another's behalf

plethora- (PLETH-ur-uh) n. an excess; an overabundance

pliable- (PLIE-uh-bul) adj. flexible; easy to bend or mold; easily influenced or persuaded

plimsolls-n. sneaker shoes

plowboy-n. (slang) a country boy

plucky-adj. brave; showing courage and energy in difficult circumstances

plug-n. (slang) a favorable public mention of a business, commercial product or artistic performance on a radio or television program

plug-ugly-n. (slang) a gangster; a rowdy individual

plum-n. a very desirable assignment, position or reward

plumage- (PLOOM-ij) n. a bird's feathers; elegant dress

plumb-vb. to measure the depth of; to examine carefully and thoroughly
adj. vertical

plunderbund-n. a group of commercial, financial or political interests that exploits the public

plutocracy- (ploo-TOK-ruh-see) n. a government or state ruled by the wealthy

pocket veto-n. an indirect veto brought about by the failure of the President to sign a presented bill within ten days before the recess of Congress

poetic justice-n. an outcome in which virtue is rewarded and evil is punished, often in an appropriate way

poetic license-n. the freedom taken by an artist or writer to depart from the standard rules of form, fact or style to achieve a desired effect

poignant- (POIN-yunt) adj. emotionally moving or touching; piercing; keen and relevant

point-blank-n., adv. plain; straightforward; direct

pointed-adj. clearly evident; referring to or directed at a specific person or thing; sharp; cutting

point man-n. someone having a crucial role at the forefront of an activity, as in a social or political movement

p

poison-pen-n. (slang) an anonymous, abusive letter or note written out of hatred or ill will in order to harass the recipient

poison pill-n. (slang) a defensive plan or tactic for preventing the unfriendly takeover of a corporation by making its acquisition prohibitively expensive

pokey-n. (slang) a jail or prison

polarize-vb. to separate into directly opposite groups or viewpoints

polemic- (puh-LEM-ik) n. a powerful argument or controversial discussion that attacks a particular doctrine or opinion

politic- (PALL-ih-tik) adj. wise, prudent and well-devised

political action committee-n. a committee formed by any special-interest group to raise money and contribute to the campaigns of political candidates whom they support

politico- (puh-LIT-ih-KOH) [Latin] n. a politician

Pollyanna-n. an excessively or foolishly optimistic individual

poltergeist- (POL-tur-GIEST) [German] n. a ghost who supposedly makes mysterious, noisy disturbances and creates disorder

poltroon- (pol-TROON) n. a complete coward

polyglot-n. a person who reads, speaks or writes in several languages

polymath-n. someone who knows a great deal about many different subjects

ponderous-adj. dull; uninteresting; lacking grace or refinement

pontificate- (pon-TIF-ih-KATE) v. to act or speak in a conceited, domineering way

Ponzi scheme- (PON-zee) [Italian] n. an illegal investment scheme in which early investors are paid artificially high returns with funds raised from later investors

pooh-bah- (POO-BAH) n. (slang) a leader or official who maintains complete control by holding many offices

pooh-pooh- (POO-POO) vb. (slang) to express contempt or scorn for; to belittle; to express impatience about

poop-n. (slang) current inside information; the relevant facts

poop sheet-n. (slang) a brief summary of facts or data about a specific subject

popinjay- (POP-in-JAY) n. a conceited, talkative person

poppycock-n. (slang) nonsense; foolish talk

populist- (POP-yuh-list) n. anyone who supports the rights, interests and views of the common people

p

pork barrel-n. (slang) government projects or spending that result in jobs or other benefits to a specific region in order to please legislators' constituents

portend-vb. to serve as a warning or forecast; to signify; to suggest

posh-adj. (slang) fashionable and luxurious; elegant

posit- (POZ-it) vb. to presume; to suggest; to position

post hoc- (HOK, HOHK) [Latin] adj., adv. in the form of an argument whereby one event is claimed to cause a later event simply by having occurred earlier

postpartum-adj. related to the period following childbirth

postprandial- (post-PRAN-dee-ul) adj. after a meal; after dinner

postulate- (POS-chuh-LATE) vb. to presume; to accept as true without proof; to claim

potboiler-n. (slang) a writing or painting hurriedly produced only for money

potpourri- (POH-poo-REE, -puh-REE) [French] n. a mixture of various things; a medley; a mixture of dried flower petals and spices used as a fragrance

potshot-n. an easy shot at close range; a random shot; a criticism made without careful thought

pound of flesh-n. a debt harshly demanded upon

powder keg-n. a potentially explosive thing or situation

powder monkey-n. (slang) one who works with explosives

power broker-n. one who exerts strong political or economic influence by virtue of the votes and individuals he or she controls

power play-n. an attempt to achieve an objective, as in business or politics, by using or threatening to use power rather than diplomacy

power politics-n. international political relations in which each nation threatens to or uses military or economic power to further its own interests

powwow-n. (slang) any conference or gathering

practicum- (PRAK-tih-kum) [Latin] n. a course in a specialized field of study in which a student gains on-the-job experience

prate-vb. to speak foolishly at length

pratfall-n. a fall on the buttocks for comic effect; a humiliating defeat, failure or error

prattle-vb. to talk childishly or foolishly

preachment-n. a long, tiresome sermon

precatory- (PREK-uh-TOR-ee) adj. relating to or expressing an appeal, request or petition

p

preciosity- (PRESH-ee-OS-ih-tee) n. extreme refinement, as in language, taste or style

precipitate- (prih-SIP-ih-TATE, pree-) vb. to cause to happen suddenly or prematurely; to hasten

précis- (PRAY-SEE, pray-) [French] n. a summary of an article or book; an abstract

predatory- (PRED-uh-TOR-ee) adj. robbing; exploiting; greedy; bloodthirsty

predilection- (PRED-uh-LEK-shun) n. a preference or partiality for something

predormition- (PREE-dor-mih-shun) n. a period of semiconsciousness before sleep

preemie- (PREE-mee) n. (slang) a prematurely-born infant

preemptive- (pree-EMP-tiv) adj. undertaken to prevent an anticipated, usually unpleasant situation or occurrence

preen-vb. to dress or groom with great care; to be proud or take satisfaction in

pregnant-adj. significant; meaningful; overflowing; creative; productive

prehensile- (pree-HEN-sil) adj. capable of grasping or holding

premonition- (PREE-muh-NISH-un, PREM-uh-) n. a warning in advance; an anticipation

preponderance- (prih-PON-dur-uns) n. majority; domination; superiority

preposterous- (prih-POS-tur-us) adj. absurd; ridiculous; foolish

presage- (PRES-ij) vb. to predict; to forecast

prescient- (PRESH-unt, PREE-shunt) adj. having knowledge of events or actions before they occur; possessing foresight

presentiment- (prih-ZEN-tuh-munt, pree-) n. a feeling that something will soon occur

pressure cooker-n. (slang) a difficult, stressful situation or environment

pressure group-n. an interest group that seeks to influence government officials and the public regarding its particular concerns and objectives

presto- [Latin] adj., adv. at once; fast; quickly

pretense-n. an instance of pretending; a false claim or reason

pretentious- (prih-TEN-shus, pree-) adj. overly self-important; claiming; pretending; showy; overdone

preterhuman-adj. beyond that which is human; superhuman

preternatural-adj. beyond that which is normal in nature; extraordinary; supernatural

pretext-n. an excuse; a cover-up; a front

P

prevaricate- (prih-VAIR-uh-KATE) vb. to lie; to speak or act in a misleading or evasive manner

prexy-n. (slang) a president, especially of a college or university

price support-n. maintenance of prices at a specific level by government purchases of surpluses

prig-n. one who is overly proper or precise in an irritating manner
vb. to steal

prim-adj. very formal and precise; neat and trim; moral

prima donna- (PREE-muh, PRIM-uh-) [Italian] n. the principal woman singer in an opera company; a conceited, temperamental person; a person who takes praise and privileged treatment as rights

prima facie- (PRIE-muh FAY-shuh, -FAY-shee) [Latin] adj., adv. at first sight; on first view; self-evident

primal- (PRIE-mul) adj. first; original; of the greatest importance

primer-n. a book that covers the basics of a subject

primeval- (prie-MEE-vul) adj. the earliest or original; ancient

primogenitor- (PRIE-moh-JEN-ih-tur) n. the earliest ancestor of a family

primordial- (prie-MOR-dee-ul) adj. first in time; original; fundamental

primp-vb. to dress or groom in a fussy way

primrose-adj. light-yellow

primrose path-n. a lifestyle of ease and pleasure; a course of action that seems easy and suitable but can actually end in disaster

prismatic- (priz-MAT-ik) adj. brilliantly colored; dazzling

prissy-adj. (slang) very prim and proper; fussy

pristine- (PRIS-TEEN, prih-STEEN) adj. pure; unspoiled; original

privation- (prie-VAY-shun) n. hardship; poverty; lack of necessities or comforts of life

privatize- (PRIE-vuh-TIZE) vb. to change a business or industry from government ownership and control to private enterprise

privy- (PRIV-ee) adj. secret; confidential

proactive- adj. acting in advance to promote or prevent a situation

probative- (PRO-buh-tiv) adj. furnishing evidence or proof; serving to test or try

probity- (PRO-bih-tee) n. complete honesty; uprightness; integrity

p

pro bono- (BOH-noh) [Latin] adj. professional services performed without
   compensation for the public good or the poor

proclivity- (pro-KLIV-ih-tee) n. a natural tendency; a predisposition; an inclination

procrustean- (pro-KRUS-tee-un) adj. tending to secure conformity to doctrines at
   any cost; drastic

prod-vb. to urge; to stir up; to poke or jab with a pointed object

prodigal- (PROD-ih-gul) adj. wastefully extravagant; reckless with money

prodigious- (pruh-DIJ-us) adj. enormous; extraordinary; marvelous

prodrome-n. an early symptom that signifies the onset of a disease

production values-n. the technical elements of a production, as in lighting and sound,
   that are used to increase audience appeal

proffer- (PROF-ur) vb. to offer; to tender

profligate- (PROF-lih-git, -gate) adj. recklessly wasteful; shamelessly immoral

pro forma- [Latin] adj. done as a formality; as a matter of form; provided in advance
   to describe form

profuse- (pruh-FYOOS, pro-) adj. plentiful; generous; extravagant; excessive

progenitor- (pro-JEN-uh-tur) n. a direct ancestor; an originator or founder of an organization or movement

progeny- (PROJ-uh-nee) n. children; descendants

prognosticate- (prog-NOS-tih-KATE) vb. to predict from available facts; to foretell

proletariat- (PROH-luh-TAIR-ee-ut) n. the industrial working class

prolix- (pro-LIKS, PRO-LIKS) adj. unnecessarily wordy; drawn out; long-winded

Promethean- (pro-MEE-thee-un) adj. boldly creative, original or innovative

promontory- (PROM-un-TOR-ee) n. a high ridge of land that extends out into a body of water

promulgate- (PROM-ul-GATE) vb. to announce officially or publicly; to make widespread; to instruct

propaedeutic- (PRO-pih-DOOT-ik) adj. providing introductory instruction

prophylactic- (PRO-fuh-LAK-tik) n., adj. protective; preventing disease

propinquity- (pruh-PING-kwih-tee, pro-) adv. nearness in place or time; similarity in nature; kinship

propitiate- (pruh-PISH-ee-ATE, pro-) vb. to make peace with; to accommodate; to soothe

p

propitious- (pruh-PISH-us, pro-) adj. favorable; gracious; kindly

proprietary- (pruh-PRIE-ih-TAIR-ee, pro-) adj. relating to an owner of property; privately owned and operated; owned by virtue of a patent, trademark or copyright

propriety- (pruh-PRIE-ih-tee, pro-) n. good manners; properness; fitness

pro rata- (RAY-tuh, RAT-uh) [Latin] adv. in proportion

prosaic- (pro-ZAY-ik) adj. ordinary; unimaginative; dull

proscribe-vb. to forbid; to prohibit; to condemn; to banish; to outlaw

proselytize- (PROS-uh-lih-TIZE) vb. to try to convert others to one's own religious faith or political belief system by using convincing argument or strongly persuasive language

prosit- (PRO-zit) interj. (used as a toast) to your health

prospective- (pruh-SPEK-tiv) adj. expected; likely; future

prosthesis- (pros-THEE-sis) n. an artificial device used to replace a missing body part, such as a limb, eye or tooth

protean- (PRO-tee-un) adj. easily changeable from one form, shape or meaning to another; having considerable diversity or variety

protectionism-n. the economic theory, policy or system of protecting domestic manufacturers by limiting, through quotas or tariffs, the importing of foreign goods and services

protégé- (PRO-tuh-zhay) [French] n. a person guided and promoted in training or career development by an influential person

protracted- (pro-TRAK-tud) adj. prolonged; drawn out

provincial- (pruh-VIN-shul, pro-) adj. narrow-minded and self-centered; limited; unsophisticated; not fashionable

proving ground-n. a place for testing new weapons, devices or theories

proviso- (pruh-VIE-zoh, pro-) [Latin] n. a clause in a document or statute that makes some condition, restriction, qualification or stipulation

provost- (PRO-VOHST) n. a high-ranking university administrator who deals with faculty and curriculum matters

prune-n. (slang) an annoying, incompetent or stupid person
vb. to trim plants or trees to improve shape or growth; to remove whatever is unnecessary or undesirable; reduce

pry-vb. to look closely or ask curiously; to snoop; to obtain with effort or difficulty

psephology- (see-FALL-uh-jee) n. the statistical evaluation of political polls or election returns

P

pseudo- (SOO-doh) adj. false; counterfeit; deceptive; pretended

psychosomatic- (SIE-koh-soh-MAT-ik) adj. relating to a disorder having physical symptoms but originating from mental or emotional causes; concerned with the influence of the mind on the body

psychotropic- (SIE-kuh-TROH-pik, -TROP-ik) adj. having an altering effect on the mind, as in behavior or perception

puce- (PYOOS) adj. purplish-brown

puckish-adj. mischievous; prankish

pudency- (PYOOD-un-see) n. modesty; prudishness

puerile- (PYOO-ur-ul, PYOOR-il) [French] adj. young; childish; immature

puffery-n. exaggerated praise or flattery, especially in advertising or publicity

pugnacious- (pug-NAY-shus) adj. combative; disposed to fights or quarrels

puissant- (PWIS-unt, PYOO-ih-sunt) [French] adj. strong; powerful

pulchritude- (PUL-krih-TOOD) n. great physical beauty and appeal

pulse-n. the noticeable emotions or feelings of the public or a specific group

pump priming-n. large governmental spending that is designed to stimulate expenditures by private industry

punchy-adj. (slang) forceful; vigorous

punctilious- (punk-TIL-ee-us) adj. overly attentive to minor details of behavior or form; precise; very exact

pundit-n. an expert in a particular field; a learned person; an authority

pungent- (PUN-junt) adj. sharp-smelling; sharp-tasting; forceful; penetrating; clever; stimulating

punitive- (PYOO-nih-tiv) adj. imposing punishment

punk-adj. (slang) of poor quality; in bad condition; characterized by unusual clothes and makeup and oddly clipped hair

purblind-adj. partly or nearly blind; slow in understanding or perceiving

purlieu- (PURL-yoo, PUR-loo) [French] n. an outlying or neighboring part of a city; the outskirts; a place one habitually visits

purloin-vb. to steal; to rob

purse strings-n. financial support or resources; control over such funds or resources

pursy- adj. short of breath, especially because of being too fat

p

purview-n. scope; range; understanding

pusillanimous- (PYOO-suh-LAN-uh-mus) adj. cowardly; fearful

putative- (PYOO-tuh-tiv) adj. supposed; commonly accepted; generally considered

putrid- (PYOO-trid) adj. rotten; foul-smelling; very unpleasant; morally corrupt

put-up-adj. (slang) planned secretly beforehand

putz- [Yiddish] n. (slang) an idiot; a fool
      vb. to waste time

pygmy- (PIG-mee) adj. insignificant; very small

pyrotechnics- (PIE-roh-TEK-niks, PIE-ruh-) n. the art of making and using fireworks; a fireworks display; a brilliant display of rhetoric or wit

Pyrrhic victory- (PEER-ik) [Greek] n. a victory gained at a tremendous cost

quack-n. a person pretending to have medical expertise in providing consultation
       and treatment; one falsely claiming to be an expert in any field; an imposter

quant- (KWONT) n. (slang) an expert in using mathematics, especially in stock
       trading and investment management

quark-n. a fundamental particle of matter

q

quasi- (KWAY-ZIE, -SIE) [Latin] adj. resembling; apparent; nearly

quick assets-n. highly liquid assets, such as cash on hand, current accounts receivable, and other assets readily convertible to cash, but excluding inventory or merchandize

quidnunc- (KWID-NUNK) [Latin] n. (slang) a busybody or gossip

quid pro quo- (KWID pro KWOH) [Latin] n. an equal exchange or substitution; something given in return; something equivalent

quintessential- (KWIN-tuh-SEN-shul) adj. being the most typical or perfect example of

quip-n. a clever, witty remark that is often prompted by a situation

quirky- (KWURK-ee) adj. peculiar; unconventional; eccentric

quisling- (KWIZ-ling) n. a traitor or collaborating spy who betrays his or her country and then serves as an official of the new government

quixotic- (kwik-SOT-ik) adj. foolishly idealistic; unrealistic; impractical

quizzical- (KWIZ-ih-kul) adj. puzzled; questioning; odd; peculiar; teasing

quodlibet- (KWOD-luh-BET) n. an academic debate, usually on a philosophical or theological issue

quotidian- (kwoh-TID-ee-un) adj. daily; ordinary; commonplace

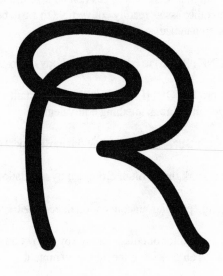

rabble-n. a noisy, disorderly crowd; the lowest class of people; a mob

rabble-rouser-n. a leader or speaker who stirs up the emotions, prejudices and
    passions of the masses

rabid- (RAB-id) adj. extremely enthusiastic; fanatic; raging; furious; uncontrollable

r

racket-n. (slang) any business, profession or occupation; an easy, profitable means of livelihood; a dishonest practice or business

raconteur- (RAK-on-TUR) [French] n. a great storyteller using humor, style and wit

racy-adj. somewhat indecent; lively; spirited; having a sharp, strong flavor or odor

raffish-adj. cheap; vulgar; in bad taste; disreputable

raft-n. (slang) a large quantity, number or collection

rag-n. (slang) a newspaper which specializes in gossip or sensationalism

ragbag-n. a collection of odds and ends; a medley

ragged edge-n. a dangerous, uncertain position; the extreme edge

raggle-taggle-adj. an odd assortment

rail-vb. to complain violently; to criticize harshly; to scold bitterly

railbird-n. (slang) a spectator at a horse race or automobile race

raillery- (RAIL-ur-ee) n. light teasing; good-natured ridicule

railroad-vb. to convict an accused person on false charges or without a fair trial; to push through rapidly to avoid careful consideration and possible criticism

raiment- (RAY-ment) n. clothing; attire; garments

rainmaker-n. (slang) an aggressive, creative developer of new business

rake-n. an immoral, lustful person

rake-off-n. (slang) a percentage or share of profits of an enterprise

ramrod-n. a harshly demanding person in charge; a strict disciplinarian

ramshackle-adj. having fallen into a state of severe disrepair; loose; shaky

ramulose- (RAM-yuh-LOHS) adj. having many small branches

rancor- (RANG-kur) n. deep-seated ill will; a bitter, continuing hatred

randy-adj. lustful; sexually uninhibited; vulgar

rank and file-n. the ordinary members of a group or organization

rankle-vb. to cause long-lasting anger or resentment; to become inflamed or sore

rapacious- (ruh-PAY-shus) adj. greedy; taking by force; predatory; plundering

rapid-fire-adj. a continuous, rapid series; performed swiftly and sharply

rapscallion- (rap-SKAL-yun) n. a rascal; a troublemaker

r

rapture- (RAP-chur) n. unequaled joy; bliss; ecstasy

rara avis- (RAIR-uh AY-vis) [Latin] n. a rare, unusual or extraordinary person or thing

rash-n. a sudden outbreak of many occurrences within a brief period
adj. reckless; ill-conceived; unduly quick

ratchet-vb. to increase or decrease in regular intervals

ratiocinate- (RASH-ee-OS-ih-NATE) vb. to reason logically and methodically

Rational Recovery-n. a substance abuse treatment program focusing on rational choice, willpower, behavior modification and individual decision-making

rat pack-n. (slang) a close group of people sharing common interests

rattlebrain-n. a silly, talkative person

rattrap-n. (slang) an unsanitary, run-down building or dwelling

ratty-adj. (slang) run-down; shabby

rave-n. (slang) an enthusiastic opinion or review

raven- (RAY-vun) adj. shiny black

rave-up-n. a lively, exciting musical performance

razzmatazz-n. (slang) excitement; a flashy display; double talk

re- (RAY, REE) [Latin] prep. concerning; in reference to

reactionary- adj. opposing progress; very conservative

ream-n. (slang) a great amount
      vb. (slang) to cheat; to deceive

receiver-n. a person appointed by a court to hold the property or funds of others
      pending litigation

recidivism- (rih-SID-ih-VIZ-um) n. a tendency to return to criminal conduct or other
      antisocial behavior

recompense- (REK-um-PENS) n. payment for services rendered; compensation for
      injury or loss

recondite- (REK-un-DITE) adj. difficult to understand; concealed; secret

reconnoiter- (REE-kuh-NOY-tur) vb. to make a preliminary survey to obtain
      information

recoup- (rih-KOOP) vb. to recover; to make up for; to receive an equivalent for

recuse- (rih-KYOOZ) vb. to disqualify or withdraw from making a decision because
      of personal interest or prejudice

r

redact- (rih-DAKT) vb. to prepare in proper form for publication; to edit

red herring-n. (slang) something drawing attention away from the central issue; a preliminary prospectus for a securities issue

redlining-n. the systematic refusal by banks and insurance companies to issue fair loans, mortgages and insurance in deteriorating neighborhoods

redolent- (RED-uh-lunt) adj. fragrant; aromatic; suggestive

reductio ad absurdum- (rih-DUK-tee-oh ad ub-SUR-dum) [Latin] n. disproving a statement by showing the absurdity or impossibility of its certain conclusion

reeling-adj. staggering; swaying; falling back

refractory- (rih-FRAK-tuh-ree) adj. stubborn; disobedient; unmanageable

rejoinder- (rih-JOIN-der) n. an answer or response; a reply

relegate- (REL-ih-GATE) vb. to assign to an inferior position; to refer a matter for decision or performance; to classify

remiss-adj. careless; negligent

remonstrate- (rih-MAHN-STRATE, REM-un-) vb. to protest; to complain; to object

remuneration- (rih-MYOO-nuh-RAY-shun) n. payment; compensation

renege- (rih-NIG, -NEG) vb. to break a promise

repartee- (REP-ur-TEE, -ar-TAY) n. a swift, clever reply; skill in making witty replies

replete- (rih-PLEET) adj. completely filled; abundantly supplied

reprisal- (rih-PRIE-zul) n. revenge; retaliation; a counterattack

reprobate- (REP-ruh-BATE) n. a very wicked, sinful or unprincipled person

resolute- (REZ-uh-LOOT) adj. firmly determined; having a fixed purpose

resounding-adj. echoing; ringing; complete; unmistakable

respite- (RES-pit) n. a brief period of relief or rest, as from work or pain; a pause

restive-adj. nervously impatient and uneasy; difficult to control; unmanageable

retinue- (RET-in-OO, -YOO) n. a group of attendants or followers of an important or high-ranking individual; an entourage

retread-n. (slang) a person who has been called back to work or service; a revision or reworking of something

retribution- (RET-ruh-BYOO-shun) n. punishment for past wrongdoing; something given or demanded in repayment; compensation

revamp- vb. to restore; to renovate; to revise

r

revelry- (REV-ul-ree) n. noisy merrymaking

reverse mortgage-n. a mortgage loan made to a homeowner by a bank in monthly installments up to the full value of the property or in one lump sum requiring no payments until the property is sold or the owner dies

revile- (rih-VILE) vb. to attack or denounce with abusive language; to scold harshly

revolving door-n. (slang) a company or organization having a high turnover of personnel; the practice in which a former employee of a government department goes to work for a private company doing business with or regulated by that department

rhapsodic- (rap-SOD-ik) adj. extremely enthusiastic; overjoyed; ecstatic

rhubarb- (ROO-BARB) n. (slang) a heated argument or discussion; a noisy quarrel

ribald- (RIB-uld) adj. amusingly vulgar or lewd; off-color

rickety-tick-adj. (slang) old-fashioned; corny

riddle-vb. to spread throughout; to affect every part of

rife-adj. widespread; occurring frequently; abundant; prevailing

riffraff-n. people regarded as disreputable or useless; trash

rig-vb. to manipulate dishonestly for personal gain; to equip or outfit; to arrange or put together in a hurried manner

right-to-work-adj. relating to state legislation that prohibits required union membership of workers

rigmarole- (RIG-muh-ROLE) n. a nonsensical, complicated set of procedures; foolish, rambling speech or writing; nonsense. Also rigamarole.

ringer-n. (slang) a person closely resembling another; a horse or player dishonestly substituted for another in a competition

rinky-dink-adj. (slang) cheap; of poor quality; worn out; unimportant

riposte- (rih-POST) [French] n. a quick, clever reply; a retaliatory action

rip-roaring-adj. (slang) lively, noisy and exciting

risque- (ris-KAY) [French] adj. bordering on being improper or indecent; off-color; daring

rite of passage-n. a ceremony, event or experience signifying an important transition in one's life

ritzy-adj. (slang) elegant; fancy; fashionable; luxurious; high-class

riveting-adj. completely absorbing one's attention; fascinating

roadshow-n. a show presented by theatrical performers on tour; the series of speeches and events accompanying a politician or political organization on tour

roan-adj. brown mixed with gray or white

roast-vb. (slang) to ridicule or criticize severely

rock-vb. to upset emotionally; to distress; to stun

rodomontade- (ROD-uh-mon-TAHD, ROH-duh-) [French] n. a bragging, self-glorifying speech

rogue- (ROHG) n. a rascal; a playfully mischievous person; an unprincipled, unreliable and deceitful person

rogue's gallery-n. a collection of the photographs of known and suspected criminals maintained in police files and used for identification

roil-vb. to disturb; to agitate; to anger; to irritate

rose-colored-adj. overly cheerful or optimistic

roué- (roo-AY) [French] n. a lustful man with the flair of a dashing romantic

rough-and-ready-adj. rough or crude but effective for a particular purpose or use

roughneck-n. (slang) a rough, crude, disorderly person

roughshod-adj. characterized by brutal force

round robin-n. a tournament, as in tennis or chess, in which each contestant plays every other participant

roustabout-n. an unskilled or temporary laborer, as on an oil field or ranch

rubberneck-vb. (slang) to gaze about or survey with curiosity or wonderment

rubber stamp-vb. (slang) to approve in a routine manner without deliberation or question

Rube Goldberg-adj. pertaining to any very complicated device, machine or scheme designed to perform an apparently simple operation

rubicon- (ROO-bih-kon) n. a point beyond which there is no return, typically resulting in an absolute commitment

rubric- (ROO-brik) n. a title or heading of a chapter or section; the name of a class or category; an established custom or procedural rule

ruck-n. the ordinary run of people or things; a large quantity, crowd or mass

ruddy-adj. reddish; rosy; healthy-looking

rueful-adj. causing sorrow, pity or compassion; regretful; dejected

ruffian- (RUF-ee-un, -yun) n. a brutal, lawless person; a hoodlum or thug; a bully

r

rufous- (ROO-fus) adj. rust-colored; brownish-red

rumbelow- (RUM-buh-loh) n. a combination of meaningless syllables that creates a feeling or mood, such as "lah-di-dah"

rumble-n. (slang) a widespread expression of discontent or unrest

ruminate- (ROO-mih-NATE) vb. to reflect on; to think over; to ponder

ruse-n. a crafty trick or scheme

rutilant- (ROOT-ih-lunt) adj. bright red

ruttish-adj. lustful

saber rattling-n. a threat to use military force; an elaborate display of military power

sacred cow-n. any person or thing not subject to criticism or attack

sacrosanct- (SAK-roh-SANGKT) adj. most sacred and holy

sad sack-n. (slang) a person who means well but is incompetent, ineffective, clumsy and constantly in trouble

safety net-n. any protection or guarantee against failure or financial loss

safety valve-n. an outlet for the release of strong emotion or energy

saffron- (SAF-run) adj. orange-yellow

saga- (SAH-guh) n. a long, detailed report; a long story of adventure or heroic deeds

sagacious- (suh-GAY-shus) adj. having penetrating judgment or insight; wise; shrewd

sage-n. a person widely respected for wisdom, judgment and experience

Saint Elmo's fire-n. a visible electrical discharge from pointed objects during an electrical storm

salad days-n. a time of youth, inexperience and innocence

salient- (SALE-yunt, SAY-lee-) adj. most notable; prominent

sallow- (SAL-oh) adj. yellowish; sickly in color or complexion

sally-n. a sudden, rushing attack; a sudden start into activity; a clever joke or display of wit; an excursion or trip

salubrious- (suh-LOO-bree-us) adj. promoting health or well-being; healthful

salvo-n. a discharge of bombs or firearms; a sudden outburst of praise or cheers; a forceful written or verbal attack

sanctimonious- (SANK-tuh-MOH-nee-us) adj. pretending to be devout or holy; self-righteous; holier-than-thou

sandbag-vb. to (slang) to deceive an opponent by deliberately playing poorly; to treat unjustly or severely

sang-froid- (sahn-FRWAH) [French] n. calmness in a difficult situation

sanguine- (SANG-gwin) adj. hopeful; optimistic; cheerful

sans- (SANZ, SAHN) [French] prep. without; lacking

sans souci- (SAHN SOO-see, sahn soo-SEE) [French] adj. carefree; without money

sap-n. (slang) a gullible person
    vb. to weaken gradually

sapient- (SAY-pee-unt) adj. wise; prudent; sensible

sappy-adj. (slang) foolish; silly; overly emotional

sartorial- (sar-TOR-ee-ul) adj. relating to men's clothing or dress; pertaining to tailors

saturation point-n. a limit beyond which something cannot be endured or continued

saturnalia- (SAT-ur-NAY-lee-uh, -ur-NAL-yuh) n. a period of wild, unrestrained feasting and merriment

saturnine- (SAT-ur-NINE) adj. gloomy; sad; sluggish

satyr- (SAT-ur, SAY-tur) n. a lustful man

saucy-adj. rude; disrespectful; stylish; energetic; boldly smart

savant- (suh-VAHNT, -VANT) n. a distinguished scholar; a very knowledgeable, learned individual

savior-faire- [French] (SAV-wahr-FAIR) n. ready knowledge of what to say or do, and when and how to say or do it; poise; sophistication

savior-vivre- [French] (SAV-wahr-VEE-vruh) n. the ability to live life well with sensible enjoyment

savvy- (SAV-ee) n. (slang) practical understanding; know-how; common sense

scabrous- (SKAB-rus, SKAY-brus) adj. rough in texture; indecent; improper; full of difficulties

scad-n. (slang) a large number or amount

scalawag- (SKAL-uh-WAG) n. (slang) a rascal; a troublemaker

scamp-n. a rascal; a mischievous person
vb. to perform in a careless, indifferent way

scandal sheet-n. (slang) a magazine or newspaper that regularly features gossip or sensationalism

scarlet- adj. brilliant red to reddish-orange; sinful; immoral

scat-n. jazz singing in which improvised, meaningless syllables are sung to a melody
vb. to leave immediately

scathing- (SKAY-thing) adj. harshly critical; severe; harmful; painful

scatterbrain-n. a person not capable of serious, concentrated or organized thinking

schism- (SIZ-um, SKIZ-) n. a division or split in an organized group or society; disharmony

schlemiel- (shluh-MEEL) [Yiddish] n. (slang) an incompetent, ineffective person who is easily deceived or commonly fails

schlepp- [Yiddish] n. (slang) a clumsy, stupid person
vb. (slang) to move with effort; to drag oneself; to carry or haul

schlock-n. (slang) anything that is cheap or inferior; trash

schlockmeister- (SHLOCK-MIE-stur) [German] n. (slang) a person who makes or deals in cheap or inferior goods or material

schlump-n. (slang) one who is stupid, boring, foolish or incompetent

S

schmaltz- [Yiddish] n. (slang) excessively emotional and empty art, music or literature

schmo- [Yiddish] n. (slang) a foolish or stupid person

schmooze- [Yiddish] vb. (slang) to gossip or talk casually

schmuck- [Yiddish] n. (slang) a stupid or clumsy person; a jerk

schnook- [Yiddish] n. (slang) a stupid or easily cheated person

schoolmarm-n. a woman teacher regarded as strict, old-fashioned or prudish

scintilla- (sin-TIL-uh) n. the least bit; a shred; a spark

scion- (SIE-un) n. a descendent or heir

scissors-and-paste- adj. (slang) relating to a literary work that is derived from another work or works

scofflaw- n. (slang) a habitual offender of the law

scoop-vb. (slang) to broadcast or publish an important news story before a competitor

scrap-vb. disregard; to abandon

scrape-n. a fight; a conflict; an embarrassing situation

screamer-n. (slang) a sensational headline

screaming meemies- (MEE-meez) n. (slang) severe nervous tension

scribe-n. an author or writer

scrupulous- (SKROO-pyuh-lus) adj. careful in deciding what is morally right;
        principled; conscientious; extremely thorough; strict

scrutinize- (SKROOT-uh-NIZE) vb. to examine very carefully and critically

scurrilous- (SKUR-uh-lus) adj. foul-mouthed; indecent; obscene; vulgar

scuttle-vb. (slang) to disregard; to abandon

scuttlebutt-n. (slang) a rumor; gossip

scut work-n. (slang) work regarded as boring, tiresome and unskilled

seamy-adj. unpleasant; disgraceful; degrading; morally low

seat-of-the-pants-adj. (slang) relying on or using experience and intuition rather
        than a method or plan; improvised

second banana-n. (slang) a show business performer who plays the straight
        man or secondary performer to the star comedian; any assistant in a
        subordinate position

second-source-adj. relating to a cooperative arrangement in which the products of
        one company are also manufactured by another company

secret society-n. an organization that conceals certain activities, such as rites of initiation, from nonmembers

sectarian- (sek-TAIR-ee-un) adj. relating to a particular group, party or religious denomination; partisan; narrow-minded; limited

security blanket-n. (slang) anything that gives one a sense of safety or eliminates anxiety

sedition- (sih-DISH-un) n. resistance to governmental authority; civil disobedience; rebelliousness

sedulous- (SEJ-uh-lus) adj. hardworking and persevering; constant

seed money-n. money given or required to begin the financing of or the start of a long-term project

seedy-adj. run-down; shabby; disreputable; unkempt

seemly-adj. suitable; proper; pleasing in appearance; handsome

seer-n. an observer; one who claims to predict a person's destiny or forecast events

segue- (SEG-way, SAY-gway) vb. to move smoothly and continuously from one condition, element or situation to another

self-abasement-n. humiliating or degrading oneself because of guilt or inferiority

self-absorbed- adj. very self-involved in one's own affairs or interests

self-aggrandizement- (uh-GRAN-diz-munt, -DIZE-munt) n. the act or practice of exaggerating or improving one's reputation, power or importance

self-deprecating- (DEP-rih-KAY-ting) adj. tending to undervalue oneself and one's talents

self-effacing- (ih-FAY-sing) adj. modest; not drawing attention to oneself

self-reproach-n. guilt feelings; blame of oneself

self-styled-adj. alleged; pretended; professed; styled or described by oneself

semantics- (suh-MAN-tiks) n. the study of the meaning and usage of words

seminal- (SEM-uh-nul) adj. creative; highly influential in an original way; essential; crucial

semiotics- (SEE-mee-OT-iks) n. the study of signs and symbols

senescent- (suh-NES-unt) adj. aging; growing old

sensationalism-n. the use of methods or material in politics, writing or journalism which are intended to excite, shock or arouse curiosity

sensitivity training-n. a type of group therapy whereby members of the group seek a deeper understanding of themselves and others by exchanging experience, feelings and physical contacts

sententious- (sen-TEN-shus) adj. self-righteous; excessively moralizing; concise

sentient- (SEN-shunt, SEN-shee-unt) adj. conscious; able to perceive by the senses

separatist- (SEP-ur-uh-tist, SEP-ruh-tist) n. a person who advocates political, racial or religious separation; one who withdraws from an established institution, cause or movement

sequacious- (sih-KWAY-shus) adj. lacking individuality in thought; dependent; compliant; following logically or smoothly; happening in a sequence

sequester- (sih-KWES-tur) vb. to set or keep apart from outside influence; to segregate; to isolate; to retire from public life

serendipity- (SAIR-un-DIP-uh-tee) n. accidental good fortune; the aptitude of making fortunate discoveries or coming upon important insights by accident

serial- (SUR-ee-ul) adj. produced or published in installments, such as a novel or television drama

seriatim- (SUR-ee-AY-tim, -OT-im) adj., adv. in a series; one after another; point by point

serpentine- (SUR-pun-TEEN, -TINE) adj. twisting; winding; crafty; cunning; snakelike

setoff-n. anything that compensates or offsets something else; a counterbalance

Seven Sisters-n. a group of women's colleges in the Northeastern U.S.; the attitudes, fashions and standards associated with their students

severable- (SEV-ur-uh-bul) adj. able to be separated; divisible into legally distinct rights or obligations

shaggy dog story-n. (slang) a long, drawn-out joke that ends with an absurd or irrelevant conclusion

shakedown-n. (slang) an extortion of money by blackmail; a thorough search of a person or place

shakeout-n. the elimination of marginal or unprofitable businesses or products because of a decline in economic activity

shake-up-n. an extensive or drastic reorganization of personnel or policy in a business or government

sham-adj. not genuine; false; counterfeit; pretended

shaman- (SHAH-mun, SHAY-) n. a contemporary guru-type who maintains religious control over a group of followers

shambles-n. a condition or scene of complete destruction or disorder

shamus- (SHAY-mus) n. (slang) a police officer or private detective

sharp-tongued-adj. harshly critical in speech

sheepish-adj. embarrassed by one's fault; shy; bashful; gentle; mild

shell company-n. an inactive public company that uses its stock to acquire a small operating company so that the smaller company can acquire a public listing on stock exchanges without having prospectuses reviewed by the Securities and Exchange Commission

shell game-n. any scheme to cheat or trick people

shelve-vb. to put aside or away; to dismiss; to retire from service

shenanigan- (shuh-NAN-ih-gun) n. mischief; nonsense; trickery; a prank

shepherd-vb. to personally direct or guide

shibboleth- (SHIB-uh-leth) [Yiddish] n. a word, phrase or custom identified with a particular group; a slogan or catchword

shiftless-adj. lazy; incapable; inefficient

shifty-adj. deceitful; sly; untrustworthy

shill-n. (slang) one who poses as an enthusiastic gambler or a satisfied customer to lure onlookers into participating in a swindle

shilly-shally-vb. to be indecisive; to hesitate; to go back and forth

shoo-in-n. (slang) a sure winner of a race or election

short list-n. a list of candidates or items that have been selected for final consideration, as in filling a position or making an award

short shrift-n. very little care or attention resulting from a lack of interest, sympathy or patience

short subject-n. a brief film shown before a feature-length film

show-and-tell-n. a public display or presentation

showpiece-n. something that is an outstanding example of its kind

showstopper-n. (slang) a performer or performance that generates so much audience applause that the show is temporarily interrupted

shrew-n. a nagging, scolding or mean-tempered woman

shtick- [Yiddish] n. (slang) an entertainment routine or gimmick; a special talent or trait that generates attention or recognition

shutterbug-n. (slang) an enthusiastic amateur photographer

shuttle diplomacy-n. diplomacy between hostile countries that is conducted by a mediator who travels frequently between the nations involved

shylock-n (slang) a loan shark; a ruthless creditor or businessman

sic-adv. intentionally written (used within brackets [sic] to show that a surprising word, phrase, mistake or fact was precisely reproduced from an original source)
vb. to pursue and attack; to urge or incite to attack; to set upon

sidebar-n. a short article printed alongside a major news story that typically presents late-breaking, contrasting or additional news

sideshow-n. something of minor importance; any subordinate event or issue

sidewalk superintendent-n. (slang) a pedestrian or onlooker at a construction or demolition site

siege mentality-n. a paranoid state of mind in which one feels under attack by hostile, external forces

sight gag-n. a comic bit or effect that depends on action rather than words

sightly-adj. visually pleasing; providing a splendid view; scenic

sight reading-vb. to read or perform something, such as unfamiliar written music, without prior preparation

signpost-n. an obvious clue; a clear indication; a symptom

silent partner-n. one who makes financial investments in a business without participating in its management

silk-stocking-adj. wealthy or upper-class; fashionably dressed

silver lining-n. a comforting or hopeful prospect in the midst of difficulty or misfortune

silver-tongued-adj. smooth-talking and persuasive

silvery-adj. having a clear, soft sound

simp-n. (slang) a foolish or simple person

simpatico- (sim-PAT-ih-KOH, -PAH-tih-KOH) [Latin] adj. compatible

sinecure- (SIN-ih-KYOOR) n. a salaried position or office that requires little or no work

sine qua non- (SIE-nee kway NON, SIN-ay kwah NOHN) [Latin] n. an essential condition or element; an absolute prerequisite

sinewy- (SIN-yoo-ee) adj. lean and muscular; stringy and tough; powerful; robust

singular- adj. unique; unusual; exceptional; peculiar; odd

sinistral- (SIN-ih-strul) adj. on or facing the left side; left-handed

sinistrodextral- (SIN-is-troh-DEK-strul) adj. moving from left to right

sinuous- (SIN-yoo-us) adj. winding or bending; not straightforward; dishonest

siren-n. a woman regarded as beautiful and seductive

situs- (SIE-tus) n. the normal location or position of something

sketchy-adj. incomplete; not detailed; presenting only major parts or points

skew-vb. to distort, misrepresent or twist the meaning of; to place or turn at an angle; to slant

skewbald-adj. having large patches of white and any other color except black

skimp-vb. (slang) to perform poorly or carelessly; to allow or give too little; to be stingy

skin game-n. a crooked gambling game; a swindle

skinflint-n. a stingy person

skinny-n. (slang) inside or confidential information; the real facts

skirt-vb. to avoid something difficult or controversial

skittish-adj. nervous; jumpy; lively; undependable

skullduggery- (skul-DUG-uh-ree) n. sneaky, dishonest behavior; trickery; craftiness

skull session-n. (slang) a meeting for discussing policy or strategy; a class session for an athletic team at which plays or strategy are studied and discussed

slant-n. a personal opinion or point of view; a bias or distortion in reporting; a quick glance

sledgehammer-adj. very powerful; ruthlessly severe; crushing

sleeper-n. a previously disregarded person or thing that achieves unexpected recognition or success

sleuth- (SLOOTH) n. (slang) a detective

slew-n. (slang) a large amount, number or group

slick-n. (slang) a popular magazine that is printed on high-quality glossy paper adj. deceptively believable or clever; smooth

slicker-n. (slang) an individual with stylish clothing and manners; a cleverly deceptive person

slighting-adj. belittling; offensive; insulting

slink-vb. to move in a quiet, sneaking manner

slippery slope-n. a tricky, problematic situation

slipshod-adj. careless or sloppy in appearance or workmanship

slithery-adj. slippery; sliding

slop-n. (slang) excessive emotion in speech or writing

slow burn-n. (slang) a gradually increasing sense or display of anger

slubber-vb. to perform carelessly and hurriedly

sluggard- (SLUG-urd) n. a habitually idle or lazy individual

slush-n. overly emotional speech or writing

slush fund-n. money raised for undesignated purposes, such as bribery, other corrupt
     practices, political pressure or entertainment

smarmy-adj. falsely flattering to gain another's favor

smart card-n. (slang) a plastic card similar to a credit card that contains a memory
     chip to enable its owner to pay bills, make banking transactions, and purchase
     various goods and services

smart money-n. (slang) money bet or invested by experienced, well-informed
     individuals

smattering-n. a small, scattered amount or number; shallow knowledge

smidgen- (SMIJ-un) n. (slang) a very small amount; a bit

smoke screen-n. anything said or done to mislead or conceal one's plans or intentions

smoking gun-n. (slang) any conclusive evidence that proves guilt or fault

smooth-tongued-adj. speaking in a polished, pleasing or persuasive manner

snafu- (snah-FOO, SNAF-oo) n. (slang) mixed up as usual; in characteristic confusion and disorder

snake in the grass-n. a deceitful person or dangerous thing that seems harmless or hidden

snake oil-n. a liquid substance having no medicinal value that is fraudulently sold to cure many ills; deceptive speech or writing

snake pit-n. (slang) a chaotic, disorderly place; a mental health facility

sneaky Pete-n. (slang) very inexpensive wine

snip-n. one who is small in size or stature; a mischievous, disrespectful person

snippet-n. a small bit or portion

snit-n. a state of anger or agitation

snivel- (SNIV-ul) vb. to cry and sniffle; to complain tearfully

snooker-vb. (slang) to fool; to deceive; to trap one into an undesirable situation

snowball-vb. to accumulate or increase rapidly in size or importance

S

snowbird-n. (slang) a northern tourist who vacations in the South during the winter

soapbox-n. a temporary platform used by one making an informal, unrehearsed speech to a street audience; a place, platform or publication used by someone to make an passionate speech or appeal

sober-adj. plain; straightforward; serious; self-restrained

sobriquet- (SOH-brih-KAY, -ket) [French] n. a nickname or assumed name

socko-adj. (slang) very impressive and effective; excellent

Socratic method- (suh-KRAT-ik, soh-) n. a method of discussion or teaching in which the meaning of a concept is analyzed and the logical soundness of a definition is examined using a series of questions and answers

soft-pedal-vb. (slang) to make less obvious; to play or tone down

soft soap-vb. (slang) to flatter; to talk smoothly

soft touch-n. (slang) one who is easily persuaded or taken advantage of

softy-n. (slang) an overly trusting or emotional person; one who lacks energy, physical stamina or the desire to punish or be strict

soigné- (swahn-YAY) [French] adj. fashionable; well-groomed; neat

soireé- (swah-RAY) [French] n. an evening party or reception

sojourn- (SOH-jurn) n. a temporary visit; a brief period of residence

solace- (SALL-is) n. comfort; relief

soldier of fortune-n. one who will serve in an army for love of adventure or personal gain; any adventurer

solecism- (SALL-ih-SIZ-um, SOH-lih-) n. a violation of established standards in usage, grammar or etiquette

solicitor general-n. a U.S. Department of Justice lawyer who represents the U.S. in cases before the Supreme Court

solicitous- (suh-LIS-uh-tus) adj. concerned; worried; willing; eager; very careful

solipsism- (SALL-ip-SIZ-um) n. the theory that the self is the only reality; the practice of extreme self-centeredness

soluble- (SALL-yuh-bul) adj. easily dissolved; capable of being explained or solved

somatic- (soh-MAT-ik) adj. relating to the body; physical

somatist- (SOH-muh-TIST) n. a psychiatrist who believes that all mental illnesses are physical in origin

somniloquy- (som-NIL-uh-kwee) n. the act or habit of talking in one's sleep

song and dance-n. (slang) a detailed explanation intended to mislead; an excessive explanation

songbird-n. a female singer

soothsayer-n. a person claiming to predict the future or foretell events

sop-n. something given as a concession, such as a bribe

sophistry- (SOF-ih-stree) n. believable but misleading argumentation or reasoning

sophomoric- (SOF-uh-MOR-ik) adj. showing immaturity and lack of judgment; juvenile

soporific- (SOP-uh-RIF-ik) adj. causing sleep; very sleepy; very boring

sordid-adj. filthy; undignified; low-down; morally degrading

sorrel- (SOR-ul) adj. a light reddish-brown

sortie- (SOR-tee) [French] n. a mission of a combat aircraft

sound bite-n. (slang) a very brief broadcast statement, such as a remark made by a politician during a news report

sounding board-n. a person or group whose reactions serve as a test for one's ideas or opinions; a means or device which helps to spread or popularize an idea or point of view

sous-chef- (SOO-) [French] n. a chef's assistant

space writer-n. a journalist or other writer who is paid according to the amount of space occupied by the copy used

spacey-adj. (slang) eccentric; offbeat; unconventional

spaghetti western-n. (slang) a low-budget film produced by the Italian movie industry about cowboys in the western U.S.

spark plug-n. (slang) a person or thing that activates or inspires an endeavor

Spartan-adj. very self-disciplined or self-restrained; brave; strict

spate-n. a sudden rush or outpouring; a large amount or number

speak-easy-n. (slang) a place where alcoholic drinks are sold illegally

spearhead-vb. to be the leader of

special assessment-n. a special tax placed on property to pay for a local public improvement that will benefit the property

specious- (SPEE-shus) adj. misleading; not genuine; deceptively attractive; seemingly reasonable but incorrect

specter-n. a ghost; a phantom; a fearful or disturbing image, object or prospect

spellbound-adj. fascinated; captivated

spendthrift-n. one who wastes money

sphere of influence-n. an area in which political or economic influence is exerted by one nation or another

sphinx-like-adj. mysterious; puzzling

spiel- (SPEEL) n. (slang) a lengthy, enthusiastic speech or argument intended to persuade or sell something

spin-n. (slang) an interpretation, especially of a politician's statements, that is designed to sway public opinion

spine-n. courage; willpower; strength of character

spinoff-n. a byproduct or new application of an activity, enterprise or process, a television series based on characters or situations from a previous series

spiny-adj. troublesome; difficult

splenetic- (splih-NET-ik) adj. irritable; bad-tempered

splinter group-n. a group that has broken away from a parent group

spoof-vb. to fool; to deceive; to joke or satirize in a playful manner

spoonerism- (SPOO-nuh-RIZ-um) n. an unintentional interchange of sounds of two or more words with clever or humorous results, as in "hing of kearts" for "king of hearts"

spoon-feed-vb. to provide knowledge or information in an oversimplified way; to pamper

spoony-adj. (slang) foolishly sentimental; overly emotional

sportive-adj. playful; fun-loving

springboard-n. anything serving as the starting point for a career or activity

spunk-n. (slang) courage; spirit

spurious- (SPYOOR-ee-us) adj. false; fake; counterfeit

spurn-vb. to reject; to refuse; to scorn

sputter-vb. to speak hurriedly in an excited or confused manner

squabble-vb. to noisily disagree over a trivial matter

squeamish- adj. easily nauseated or upset; easily offended or shocked; oversensitive

squeeze-n. financial pressure caused by decreasing economic margins or shortages;
a girlfriend; a lover
vb. to oppress with unreasonable, burdensome demands; to obtain by
dishonest means

squeeze play-n. (slang) pressure or force exerted to achieve some goal

squelch-vb. (slang) to silence or suppress completely and convincingly

squib-n. a short, often witty or attacking article in a newspaper or magazine;
a short news item or filler

squirrel-vb. to hide; to store; to hoard

squire-vb. accompany as an escort

stagflation- (stag-FLAY-shun) n. an economic condition of sluggish economic
growth together with a high rate of inflation and unemployment

staid-adj. serious; steady and settled; rigid

stanch- (STAHNCH) vb. to stop the flow of blood; to lessen; to diminish

standard-bearer-n. an outstanding leader or chief representative of a political party,
movement or organization

standing-n. reputation, status or position in a profession or society; duration;
the right or capacity to begin a lawsuit

standpat-adj. (slang) resisting change; conservative

star-crossed-adj. unlucky; ill-fated

stargaze-vb. to daydream

starry-eyed-adj. unrealistic; impractical; overly optimistic

statuesque- (STACH-oo-ESK) adj. tall and well-proportioned; graceful; dignified

stave off-vb. to hold or put off; to evade; to repel

stay-n. a delay or postponement in legal proceedings

stealthy-adj. undercover; underground; sly; sneaky

steel blue-adj. medium grayish blue; metallic blue

steel gray-adj. bluish-gray

steel-trap-adj. very quick and keen; piercing; penetrating

steely-adj. severe; strong; mighty; unbending; bluish-gray

steering committee-n. a committee that sets the schedules or agendas of businesses or organizations

stem-vb. to stop or check the flow of; to prevent; to limit

stentorian- (STEN-tor-ee-un) adj. very loud

sterling-adj. excellent; of the highest quality

stew-vb. to worry; to be troubled or agitated; to perspire excessively

sticking point-n. an issue or point that causes action or negotiations to deadlock

stickler-n. something difficult or puzzling; one who demands exact observance of
        detail; a perfectionist

stick-to-itiveness-n. (slang) persistence

sticky-adj. (slang) difficult; painful; awkward; delicate

sticky wicket-n. (slang) a difficult or embarrassing problem or situation

stiff-necked-adj. stubborn; inflexible

stilted-adj. inflated; stuffy; overblown; high-sounding

stinkpot-n. (slang) a motorboat

stint-n. an assigned portion or period of work; a task; a restriction; a limitation

stipulate- (STIP-yoo-LATE) vb. to require by contract; to specify; to make express conditions

stir-crazy-adj. (slang) restless or crazed from a long confinement, as in a prison

stirring-adj. emotionally moving; gripping; inspiring; active; busy

stock parking-n. a financial maneuver in which the true ownership of a stock is concealed by having one investor buy and hold it under his or her name until the real owner who financed the transaction gives a direction to sell

stodgy- (STOJ-ee) adj. dull; uninteresting; unattractive; old-fashioned; solidly built; stuffy

stoic- (STOH-ik) adj. indifferent or not affected by pressure, pain, joy, grief, fortune or misfortune; unemotional

stolid- (STALL-id) adj. unemotional; unexcitable; dull

stonewall-vb. (slang) to refuse to answer or cooperate; to engage in delaying tactics; to stall

stony-adj. unfeeling; unemotional; hardhearted

stooge-n. (slang) a straight man to a comedian; someone whose actions are controlled by another; a puppet

stool pigeon-n. (slang) an informer or decoy; a spy for the police

stopgap-n. a person or thing serving as an improvised or temporary substitute

strained-adj. characterized by great emotional tension or exertion; forced; unnatural

straits-n. a crisis; an emergency; a position of desperate need or difficulty

straw-adj. yellowish

strawberry blond-adj. reddish-blond

straw boss-n. (slang) a supervisor who has little or no authority to support his or
          her orders

straw man-n. a person of little importance; an argument or opponent set up so
          as to be easily defeated or refuted; one set up as a cover or a front for
          a questionable activity or enterprise

straw vote-n. an unofficial vote or poll that indicates the trend of public opinion

stream of consciousness-n. a literary technique presenting the feelings and thoughts
          of a character in a natural, random sequence

stricture- (STRIK-chur) n. a limitation or restriction; sharp, negative remarks
          or criticism

stringer-n. a freelance or part-time correspondent for a magazine or newspaper

stroke-vb. (slang) to flatter or persuade in order to win over or restore to confidence

strong-arm-adj. (slang) using physical force; violence or coercion

strongman-n. a political leader or dictator who exercises control and leadership by force

strong suit-n. an activity, quality or skill in which a person excels

studied-adj. carefully planned; deliberate; learned; knowledgeable

stuffed shirt-n. (slang) a conceited, pompous and inflexible person

stump-n. (slang) a place or occasion used for campaign or political speeches

stupefy- (STOO-puh-FIE) vb. to daze; to make numb; to amaze; to astonish

stymie- (STIE-mee) vb. to get in the way of; to block; to frustrate; to hinder

suasion- (SWAY-zhun) n. persuasion

subaltern- (sub-ALL-turn) adj. subordinate; lower in position or rank; inferior

subjacent- (sub-JAY-sunt) adj. situated underneath or below; underlying

subjugate- (SUB-juh-GATE) vb. to conquer; to overpower; to dominate; to enslave

sublimate (SUB-lih-MATE) vb. to purify; to refine; to transform or channel an unacceptable impulse into socially acceptable activity

s

sublime-adj. grand; splendid; noble; lofty; celebrated

subliminal- (sub-LIM-uh-nul) adj. below the threshold of conscious perception or awareness

subornation- (SUB-or-NAY-shun) n. the crime of causing another to commit perjury

substantive- (SUB-stun-tiv) adj. real; having substance; essential; solid

subsume- (sub-SOOM) vb. to include within a larger general category or class

subterfuge- (SUB-tur-FYOOJ) n. an action, device or plan used to avoid or conceal something

succor- (SUK-ur) n. aid; relief; assistance

sufferable-adj. that which can be tolerated, endured or permitted

sugarcoat-vb. to make something more appealing or acceptable

sui generis- (SOO-ee JEN-ur-is, SOO-eye-) [Latin] adj. one of a kind; unique

sui juris- (SOO-ee JOOR-is, SOO-eye-) [Latin] adj. able to manage one's own affairs; of legal age and sound mind

suitor-n. a man courting a woman; one who requests or petitions; a person or group trying to purchase controlling interest in a company

sully-vb. to soil; to tarnish; to smear; to disgrace

superannuated- (SOO-pur-AN-yoo-AY-tid) adj. retired because of old age; outdated; old-fashioned

supercilious- (SOO-pur-SIL-ee-us) adj. overbearingly proud; arrogant; too self-important

Superfund-n. a U.S. government fund created for the cleanup or elimination of various toxic waste dump sites

supernal- (soo-PUR-nul) adj. heavenly; divine; above ordinary human existence

supplant- (suh-PLANT) vb. to replace; to remove; to displace

sure-fire-adj. (slang) sure to be successful; bound to perform as expected

surfeit- (SUR-fit) n. an excess; excessive eating or drinking

surmise- (sur-MIZE) vb. to guess; to imagine; to presume

surplusage- (SUR-pluh-sij) n. an excess; a surplus; an excess of words or matter

surrealistic- (suh-REE-uh-LIS-tik) adj. bizarre; weird; unreal; freakish

surreptitious- (SUR-up-TISH-us) adj. secret; undercover; sneaky; crafty

surrogate- (SUR-uh-GIT, -GATE) adj. substitute; replacement

suspense account-n. a temporary account whereby charges and credits are temporarily entered until their proper resolution can be determined

Svengali- (sven-GAH-lee) [French] n. a person who tries to dominate another, usually with evil or selfish motives

swami- (SWAH-mee) [Hindu] n. a Hindu religious teacher; a learned person

swan song-n. the final appearance or creative work of an artist, poet or musician

sway-n. (slang) stolen money or property; a large number or amount

sweatbox-n. (slang) a confining place where a person sweats; an interrogation room

sweat-equity-n. hard work put into a business or house to increase its value

sweeten-vb. (slang) to increase the value of collateral for a loan; to improve the financial desirability of an offer

sweetheart contract-n. a contract arranged by an agreement between an employer and union officials with terms disadvantageous to union members

swimmingly-adv. easily and with great success

swindle sheet-n. (slang) an expense account

switch-hitter-n. (slang) one who is skilled in two different jobs, roles or specialties; a bisexual

swoon-n. a fainting spell; a blackout; a state of great joy and pleasure

sybarite- (SIB-uh-RITE) n. a person who pursues luxury and pleasure

sycophant- (SIK-uh-funt) n. an individual who ambitiously flatters wealthy, influential people in order to win favor and thereby improve his or her own status

sylph- (SILF) n. a slender, graceful woman or girl

symbiosis- (SIM-bee-OH-sis, -bie-OH-sis) n. a mutually beneficial or dependent relationship

sympathy strike-n. a strike by a group of workers in support of another group on strike

synecdoche- (sih-NEK-duh-kee) n. a figure of speech in which a part is substituted for the whole, as in "bread" for "food", the specific for the general, an individual for a class, a material for a product made from it, or the reverse of any of these

synergy- (SIN-ur-JEE) n. cooperative activity or a combination of forces that has a greater total effect than the sum of individual effects

syrupy-adj. overly sweet in manner or tone; overly emotional; overdone

systemic- (sis-TEM-ik) adj. affecting an entire organism or body

systems analysis-n. the study of an activity or procedure using mathematics to determine its desired goal and the most efficient means of attaining it

table-vb. to postpone the discussion or consideration of

tailspin-n. a state of increasing depression or confusion; an emotional collapse

take-n. a point of view; an interpretation; an understanding

take-no-prisoners-adj. highly determined and uncompromising

talking head-n. (slang) a person on a television documentary or news show who is shown speaking at length with only the head and upper body visible

taupe- (TOHP) adj. brownish-gray

tautology- (tau-TALL-uh-jee) n. needless repetition of the same idea in different words; redundancy

tawny-adj. brownish-yellow; tan

teaching fellow-n. a graduate student in a college or university who is awarded a grant in exchange for teaching duties

teal-adj. dark bluish-green

teeming-adj. overflowing; abounding; filled with

telegenic- (TEL-uh-JEN-ik) adj. having a highly appealing physical appearance and personal qualities on television

tempestuous- (tem-PES-choo-us) adj. stormy; turbulent; violent; fierce; intense

tempus fugit- (FYOO-jit) [Latin] time flies

tendentious- (ten-DEN-shus) adj. advancing a certain point of view; biased

tenderfoot-n. a beginner; any inexperienced person; a newcomer to rough outdoor life

tenet- (TEN-it) n. a doctrine, belief or principle held as true by a group or organization

ten-strike-n. (slang) a remarkably successful action

terra cotta- (TAIR-uh KOT-uh) [Latin] adj. brownish-orange

terra firma- (TAIR-uh FUR-muh) [Latin] n. solid ground

testy-adj. irritable; touchy; impatient

tete-a-tete- (TATE-uh-TATE) [French] n. a private conversation between two people

T-Group-n. a training group

thespian- (THES-pee-un) n. an actor or actress
    adj. dramatic

think piece-n. (slang) a newspaper or magazine article consisting of background material, news analysis and personal opinions

think tank-n. (slang) a group or institute organized by a business or government to do intensive research, problem solving and theoretical study in the areas of social policy, political strategy and technology

thin-skinned-adj. easily offended or oversensitive to criticism or insults

thorny-adj. painfully controversial; difficult; annoying

threadbare-adj. worn-out; shabby; overused; stale

three-card monte-n. a gambling game in which a dealer shows a player three cards, then turns them face down and shifts them around, and then the player bets on the location of a particular card

thumbnail-adj. brief and to the point; very small

ticky-tacky-adj. cheaply built; characterized by dull, unimaginative uniformity

tide-n. a strong trend or tendency

tiff-n. a petty dispute or quarrel; a fit of irritation

time bomb-n. any potentially disastrous situation or destructive person

time warp-n. the condition or process of distorting the flow of time to suspend its passage or shift events from one time period to another

tinderbox-n. a potentially explosive or highly dangerous place or situation

tizzy-n. a state of confusion or nervous excitement

toady-n. one who flatters others for self-serving reasons

tome-n. a large, scholarly book; any volume of a work of several volumes

tomfoolery-n. foolish behavior; nonsense

t

tonsorial- (tahn-SOR-ee-ul) adj. pertaining to a barber or barbering

tony-adj. (slang) luxurious; expensive; stylish; fashionable

top banana-n. (slang) the most important person of a group or project

top-drawer-adj. (slang) of the highest standing, excellence, importance or rank

top-heavy-adj. having too many administrators or executives

topical- (TOP-ih-kul) adj. of current or local interest; contemporary

toponym- (TOP-uh-NIM) n. a name derived from a place or region,
    as in "Indiana Jones"

topsy-turvy-adj., adv. in a confused or disordered condition; upside-down

torchbearer-n. a person who communicates knowledge, inspiration or truth to others;
    an inspirational leader of a movement

torch song-n. a popular emotional song expressing sadness, hopeless yearning or
    lost love

torpedo-vb. to destroy completely

touch-and-go-adj. dangerous and uncertain; risky

touche- (too-SHAY) [French] interj. an expression used to acknowledge a successful point in debate or effective criticism

touchstone-n. an excellent example or standard for determining value or genuineness

tour de force- [French] n. an achievement of remarkable strength, skill, performance or creativity

traipse- (TRAYPS) vb. to walk about aimlessly

travail- (truh-VALE, TRAV-ALE) n. very hard physical or mental exertion; distress; agony

treadmill-n. any monotonous activity, work or routine that is seemingly endless

treasure-trove-n. a valuable discovery

trial balloon-n. an idea or plan advanced to test public opinion on an issue

tripe-n. (slang) anything worthless; nonsense

troglodyte- (TROG-loh-DITE, TROG-luh-) n. a person who lives alone in a primitive, reactionary fashion

troika- (TROY-kuh) n. a ruling body of three; any group of three

Trojan- (TROH-jun) n. a person with heroic qualities such as strength, determination, endurance and courage

t

troubadour- (TROO-buh-DOOR) n. a strolling musician or singer

troupe- (TROOP) n. a company of actors, dancers or singers

trouper-n. a reliable, hard-working, uncomplaining person; a veteran actor or performer

trump card-n. a valuable resource to be utilized at the appropriate time

trumped-up-adj. false; fabricated

trumpery- (TRUM-puh-ree) n. nonsense; deception; worthless items; junk

trumpet-vb. to announce or proclaim loudly

trunk show-n. a traveling collection of designer clothing or jewelry that is displayed in various stores

tryst- (TRIST) n. an agreement between lovers to meet at a specified time and place

turncoat-n. a traitor

tutelage- (TOOT-uh-lij) n. instruction; teaching; the state of being under a tutor or guardian

twaddle-n. foolish, silly talk or writing; nonsense

twerp-n. (slang) an insignificant, ridiculous person

twit-n. (slang) a foolishly annoying person

tyro- (TIE-roh) n. an amateur; a beginner

ubiquitous- (yoo-BIK-wih-TUS) adj. existing or seeming to exist everywhere
    at the same time

uncanny-adj. extraordinary; astounding; mysterious; strange; weird

undaunted-adj. courageous; persevering; fearless

underbelly-n. a vulnerable or unprotected area; a weak part

undercurrent-n. an underlying, hidden force, opinion or tendency

underemployed-adj. inadequately employed, as in low-skilled, poorly paid jobs
  or part-time work when one needs and desires full-time employment

underpinning-n. an underlying cause or principle; a support or foundation

underscore-vb. to emphasize or stress

under-the-counter-adj., adv. illegal or unethical and performed secretly, as in a
  clerk selling illicit drugs from behind the counter in a convenience store

undertow-n. a feeling or thought tending to run contrary to what seems the strongest

universal donor-n. a person who has type O blood and is thus able to donate blood
  to individuals in any other blood group in the ABO system

unlettered-adj. ignorant; illiterate; unsophisticated

unsung-adj. not honored or praised; uncelebrated

unswerving-adj. straight-ahead; constant; steady

untoward-adj. improper; unfavorable; troublesome

untrammeled-adj. unlimited; unrestrained

u

unwitting-adj. unaware; unintentional; inadvertent

unwonted-adj. unusual; uncommon; unique

upbeat-adj. (slang) optimistic; happy; lively

up-market-adj. appealing to or designed for high-income consumers; upscale

uppity- (UP-ih-tee) adj. (slang) arrogant; overbearing; snobbish

upshot-n. the outcome

upside down- adj., adv. disordered; confused; chaotic

upstage-vb. to draw attention or praise to oneself at another's expense; to treat in an inferior manner

upstart-n. a newly rich, powerful person, usually with a self-glorifying demeanor

valetudinarian- (VAL-ih-TOOD-ih-NAIR-ee-un) n. a person who is constantly
and nervously concerned about his or her own health

vamoose- (vuh-MOOS) vb. (slang) to leave quickly; to quit

vamp-n. (slang) a woman who exploits or seduces men
vb. to repair; to refurbish; to put together; to improvise

vanguard-n. the leading people or position in a movement or trend

vaporware-n. new software that has been announced but not yet produced

V

variety meat-n. meat other than flesh, such as liver or sweetbreads

varletry- (VAR-lih-tree) n. a disorderly crowd; a mob

vaunted-adj. highly publicized; boasted

veneer- (vuh-NEER) n. any attractive, but deceptive appearance or display; a facade

verbiage- (VUR-bij, VUR-bee-ij) n. wordiness; a style of expression

verbicide- (VUR-bih-side) n. a deliberate distortion of the meaning of a word

vermilion- (vur-MIL-yun) adj. bright red to reddish-orange

vertigo- (VUR-tih-GOH) n. severe dizziness; a state of mental confusion or disorientation

verve- (VURV) n. enthusiasm; liveliness; vigor

vestige- (VES-tij) n. a last trace or remaining bit of something

vest-pocket-adj. very small; compact

vicissitude- (vih-SIS-ih-TOOD) n. a sudden, unexpected change or variation in fortune, activities or surroundings

vie-vb. to compete; to challenge; to strive for

vignette- (vin-YET) [French] n. a short literary sketch or description; a short, memorable scene from a movie or play

vigorish- (VIG-ur-ish) n. (slang) a charge placed on bets by a bookie or gambling establishment; excessive interest paid to a moneylender

vinegary- (VIN-ih-gree, -guh-ree) adj. unpleasant; ill-tempered

virago- (vih-RAH-goh, -RAY-goh) n. a fierce-tempered woman

vis-a-vis- (VEE-zuh-VEE) [French] prep. compared with; in relation to; opposite to

visceral- (VIS-ur-ul) adj. intuitive; instinctive; emotional

vision quest-n. a religious practice that requires followers to undergo fasting, isolation and introspection to attain guidance and knowledge from supernatural forces

vita- (VEE-tuh, VIE-) [Latin] n. a brief biography or autobiography; a resume

voice-over-n. script text which is read or spoken by a movie actor or television commentator who doesn't appear on camera and which is later played over relevant video or film sequences

vulgate-n. a generally accepted version of a literary work

vulpine-adj. relating to a fox; sly; cunning; crafty

vulture fund-n. an investment vehicle that buys bonds or shares in heavily encumbered or debt-burdened companies or properties

wacky-adj. (slang) eccentric; irrational; crazy; foolish; silly

waffle-vb. (slang) to talk, write or act evasively or indecisively

wag-n. a humorous, witty individual; a joker

waif- (WAYF) n. anything that is found and unclaimed; a homeless person; an abandoned child

waiting game-n. a strategy in which advantage is sought by using delaying tactics

wake-up call-n. a significant event, situation or report that brings an issue to immediate attention

walk-through-n. a theatrical rehearsal in which the action is played out as the lines are read; a television rehearsal in which scripts are read or cameras are not used

wallah wallah-n. the person in charge; the boss

wallflower-n. (slang) a company, industry or security unfavorable with investors

Walter Mitty-n. an ordinary individual who escapes from boring reality through fantastic daydreams of personal triumph

wanton- adj. cruel and inhumane; excessive; unjustifiable; immoral; lustful

war chest-n. a fund of individual contributions created for a particular purpose

war cry-n. a phrase or slogan used to rally support for a certain cause

warhorse-n. (slang) a veteran of many conflicts or struggles, especially of military or political life

W

wash-n. (slang) an activity or enterprise that yields neither noticeable gain nor loss
vb. to undergo successful testing

waspish-adj. bad-tempered; easily annoyed or irritated

wastrel- (WAY-strul) n. one who wastes things, including money; a lazy person

watchdog-n. a person or group acting as a guardian against waste and unethical or
illegal practices

watchword-n. a rallying cry or slogan of a group or political party

watering place-n. a health resort or spa with mineral springs for bathing or consumption

waterloo-n. a disasterous or final, decisive defeat

watershed-n. a crucial turning point serving as a change of course or a dividing line

wayfarer-n. one who travels to various places on foot

waylay-vb. to wait for and attack; to ambush; to intercept in an attempt to speak with

ways and means-n. methods and means, especially legislation, for raising money
needed by a government

way station-n. a station between principal stations on a route

weak-kneed-adj. lacking courage, determination or strength of character

wedge issue-n. a controversial political campaign issue, such as reducing social security benefits, that can symbolically "drive a wedge" between different voting segments of the opposing party

wellhead-n. a principal source

well-heeled-adj. rich; wealthy; prosperous

wellspring-n. a source of continual, plentiful supply

welter-n. confusion; turmoil

wet blanket-n. (slang) one whose influence or presence diminishes the enjoyment or enthusiasm of others

whammy-n. (slang) an evil spell or jinx for subduing an adversary; a hex

whipping boy-n. one taking blame for others; a scapegoat

whipsaw-vb. to defeat in two ways at once

whirlwind-adj. very rapid; rushed

whispering campaign-n. the dissemination of defamatory rumors by word of mouth to discredit a political candidate, cause or group

whistle blower-n. (slang) one who discloses wrongdoing within an organization to those in positions of authority or to the public

W

white book-n. an official government report bound in white

white elephant-n. (slang) anything rare or expensive that is a financial burden to maintain; an activity or venture that proves to be a total failure

white goods-n. household linens, as in towels, sheets and pillowcases; large household appliances

white heat-n. intense emotion or excitement

white knight-n. a rescuer; a savior; an individual or company that prevents an unfavorable, unwanted takeover attempt by offering better terms to buy the targeted company

white knuckle-adj. (slang) characterized by tense fear or nervousness

white-livered-adj. cowardly

white paper-n. an official report of the U.S. Government about a particular issue; any in-depth, authoritative report

white slavery-n. forced prostitution

whitewash-vb. (slang) to conceal the faults or failures of; to defeat an opponent overwhelmingly

whodunit- (hoo-DUN-it) n. (slang) a mystery novel or play

wig out-vb. (slang) to become excited, upset or crazy

wildcat-adj. financially risky or unsound; occurring without official authorization, as in a labor strike

wild-eyed-adj. passionate; extreme; impractical; foolish

willies-n. (slang) nervousness; the jitters

willy-nilly-adj., adv. whether desired or not; uncertain; disordered; haphazard

windbag-n. (slang) one who talks excessively without saying much of interest or importance

window-dressing-n. a display of retail merchandise in store windows to attract customers; actions or statements made to create a falsely favorable impression or to improve appearances

winsome-adj. charming; pleasing; delightful

wirepuller-n. (slang) one who uses private influence, secret means or underhand activity for personal gain

wiseguy-n. a gangster

wistful-adj. longing; wishful; yearning

w

witch-hunt-n. (slang) an intensive investigation undertaken to harass and undermine political opposition

withering-adj. tending to destroy or overwhelm; devastating

wittol-n. a man who tolerates his wife's infidelity

wizened- (WIZ-und) adj. dried up; shriveled

wonk-n. (slang) a student who studies very hard

wooden-adj. stiff and unnatural; spiritless; clumsy; awkward

wordsmith-n. an expert on words; one who develops new words; a professional writer who uses language skillfully

workfare-n. a government welfare program requiring employable welfare recipients to register for work, enter a work training program, or perform public-service work

work-up-n. a complete patient medical examination, including a case history and laboratory tests

worldbeater-n. (slang) one having the capabilities to be superior to others in achieving great success

worrywart-n. (slang) one who worries excessively and unnecessarily

wrack-vb. to destroy; to ruin

wrinkle-n. (slang) a clever idea, device or method that is new and different;
         an ingenious innovation

wry-adj. ironically humorous; distorted; abnormally bent or twisted to one side

Xanadu- (ZAN-uh-DOO) n. a naturally peaceful, beautiful place

xanthous- (ZAN-thus) adj. yellowish

xenophobia- (ZEN-uh-FOH-bee-uh, ZEE-nuh-) n. a fear, mistrust or hatred of
        foreigners or strangers or anything foreign or strange

xeric- (ZUR-ik) adj. pertaining or adapted to an extremely dry environment

yahoo- (YAH-hoo, YAY-) n. (slang) a noisy, uneducated, unrefined person

yellow journalism-n. journalism that exaggerates or exploits the news to create
    sensations and attract or influence readers

yen-n. a strong desire or longing

y

yenta- (YEN-tuh) [Yiddish] n. (slang) a nosy, gossipy woman; a busybody

yeoman- (YOH-mun) n. a hard-working, dependable worker

yes man-n. (slang) one who gives complete approval to a superior's statements, opinions or suggestions

yokel- (YOH-kul) n. (slang) an unsophisticated country person; a country bumpkin

Young Turk-n. a young, progressive member of a political party or organization seeking to take control from an established, usually conservative group of older people

yutz- [Yiddish] n. (slang) a stupid or incompetent individual

zany- (ZAY-nee) adj. bizarre and comical; ridiculous; absurd; clownish

zealot- (ZEL-ut) n. an extreme adherent of a cause or position; a fanatic

Zeitgeist- (ZIET-GIEST) [German] n. the spirit of the times; the intellectual, moral and cultural climate of a certain era

zephyr- (ZEF-ur) n. a gentle breeze

zeppelin- (ZEP-uh-lin, ZEP-lin) n. a large airship having a rigid, cigar-shaped body

zero hour-n. (slang) any critical moment; the scheduled time for the start of an action or operation, especially a military invasion

ABOUT THE AUTHOR

NICK CAMAS, an avid wordsmith, was educated as a lawyer and has worked as a recording studio piano player. He is single and enjoys piano, reading, golf and cycling

ORDER INFORMATION

Additional copies of this book may be ordered from
your local bookstore or by calling (800) 247–6553.

Check, money order or credit card accepted. (Visa,
Mastercard and Discovery). Make your check
payable to Pennhills Press.

Please include $2.50 for postage and handling for the
first book and $1.50 for each additional book.

ISBN: 0–9645851–1–1